C000062255

Tracking with Jack

WONDERFUL WILTSHIRE

Jacky Parker

First Edition March 2019

Published by Rick Dixon (Cricklade)
19 North Wall, Cricklade, Wiltshire SN6 6DU

Design, Map and Layout by Rick Dixon

Printed by: Pixartprinting S.p.A. Italy

ISBN 978-1-9164618-1-9

Contents

Dedication

To Ed

Who dutifully drove me all through Wiltshire so that I could tread the county's pleasant pathways.

My thanks to Sandy and Chloe who gave so much constructive advice as I set out to record my adventures while exploring Wonderful Wiltshire.

AN UNSPOILED VILLAGE CALLED PURTON

In 2013 I retired from teaching and boarding education and, together with Ed my husband, set up home in Purton, a north Wiltshire village, bordering the large town of Swindon. Stepping into a new world of freedom was strange but certainly exciting. After over 45 years of living with bells, routines, time restraints and institutional procedures, I was now at liberty to map my own destiny.

And what had the world opened up to me? Nothing less than the opportunity to venture out and explore the glories of the past, set in wonderful country and urban locales.

The obvious place to begin my journey was in Purton itself because the village abounds, not only in history but in mysterious antiquity. Flint tools dating back to the Neolithic period around 3500 BC have been found at Ringsbury Camp, which was an Iron Age hill fort built about 50 BC. Roman civilisation also reached Purton, and the most exciting find was four Pottery kilns on a housing site at Dogridge in the village. Equally exciting was a walled Roman cemetery found behind the Union Workhouse. Only 13 of these have been discovered in England, so the Purton site is of immense importance.

Hypocaust Heating Tiles
The Hypocaust or system of under-floor heating was commonly used in Roman villas in Britain. These tiles found at Dogridge in 1975, were used to build pillars to support the floors.

Who knows what value the village of Purton held for the Romans during their almost 400 years of occupation in Britain? But we can easily guess that close proximity to the important Roman town of Corinium (Cirencester) and Cricklade would inevitably bring them into a circle of control.

In the late 600s it is recorded in the charters of Malmesbury Abbey that Chedwalla, the Saxon King called the village 'Piriton', 'Periton', Puriton' or 'Pirton', all of them various ways of spelling the 'Peartree Village'. It may seem odd that a whole village could be given to an individual, but in those days all land was owned by the clergy or a small number of lords.

The Normans, after their conquest in 1066, quickly took control of England and methodically made their presence felt. Purton is recorded in the Domesday Survey of 1086 as having lands for 24 ploughs. It listed Manor land, village numbers, smallholdings, cottagers, a mill and a wood of 3 square miles. A comprehensive assessment of village merit and substance! At this time there was probably a small Saxon church on the site of the present 13th century Parish Church.

Driving speedily along the High Street, as many travellers do, one might get the feeling of an austere and sombre thoroughfare. But this is far from the truth. You really need

to walk along the road and experience the fascination of the old stone buildings in the High Street, which bear witness to the passing times of Tudor, Stuart, Victorian and even modern influence.

Many of the well-established houses in the High Street are positioned on the brow of a hill overlooking Cricklade and the Thames floodplain. It is a stunning view!

Purton Museum is located above the library in what used to be the Workmen's Institute and, while a fascinating building in its own right, the museum itself is really worth a visit. It is currently open on Wednesday afternoons and Saturday mornings, though closed in winter months. Photographs and artefacts of the old village along with 1st and 2nd World War memorabilia give a nostalgic and sobering taste of bygone days.

The Angel Pub is a well-loved meeting place for many of the local folk, and, according to records, has been an important part of village life for several centuries. The current building dates back to 1704 and legend has it that 6000 gallons of its locally brewed beer were consumed during an 18th century Purton fair. I guess there must have been a few sore heads after that celebration! In times past the Angel *(right)* made a name for itself with the lure of their Sunday pub lunches, and past reviews reflected the high standard of good home cooked food, with an abundance of vegetables and always a crisp, traditional Yorkshire pudding. Lunches are still available, but booking is essential.

A friendly atmosphere and a warm open fire are strong draw cards for both the locals and the casual visitor.

The Royal George *(left)* re-opened for a brief while under new management attracting a strong following of the local community. We have hopes it may open again. Although documents for this pub go back to 1808, it is thought that the building might be older.

The landlord and landlady assured me that the timbered roof in the annexe section comes from broken wreckage of the Royal George which sank in 1782 while undergoing repairs in Portsmouth Harbour. It is estimated that 1200 people were on board on that fateful 29 August and that 900 perished when the ship heeled over during the repair process. I suppose that it is good we can, in some small way, remember a part of history, even if it was filled with tragedy.

> *Toll for the brave*
> *The Brave that are no more,*
> *All sunk beneath the wave,*
> *Fast by their native shore.*

> *William Cowper, The Loss of the Royal George, 1782*

Although clientele are rich in praise for The Bell at Purton Stoke, it did not always enjoy the same admiration and approval in its early years. Reckless, rowdy and wayward behaviour must have prompted the authorities to prosecute the landlord in 1844 for keeping a house of ill repute.

The Bell *(right)* later became a popular meeting place for the Purton Stoke community and now its good name draws visitors from far afield. Web site reviews praise the quality of the food, the welcoming atmosphere, the traditional pub ambience and the friendly staff; and without exception, guests promise to return.

The Pear Tree hotel *(below)* was once an obvious choice for travellers who enjoy fine wine, and good dining. Sadly, it has recently closed down and we all live in hopes that its previous tasty cuisine will once more become available and that it will return to

embody the charm of being an old world Country House with a fascinating history.

Previous owners who bought it in 1987 from the Diocese of Bristol explained that the present establishment was once the vicarage and was originally sited in the churchyard. Encroaching graves made a move obligatory and so, in 1911, stone by stone the old house was laboriously carted to its present location.

Languishing in a poor state of repair, the later owners battled their way through red tape of planning and historical complications and lovingly converted the old premises into a charming Country House. With energy and enthusiasm, they set out to provide for the traveller the best service, cuisine and restful experience possible. Their web site reviews showed a host of grateful customers who thoroughly enjoyed the Pear Tree experience.

One of our most illustrious houses in the High Street is College Farm House *(right)*. It was once a dwelling place of the eminent Edward Hyde, Earl of Clarendon, who was a distinguished statesman and historian and served Charles I as an adviser, and Charles II during his exile.

In 1658 he was appointed Lord Chancellor by Charles II and, on the Restoration of the Monarchy, returned to England with the king. His daughter Anne may have spent some of her childhood at College Farm House and in 1660 she secretly married the king's brother (later James II). Although she died before James ascended the throne, her two daughters, Mary and Anne were to become future Queens of England, Scotland and Ireland.

While in conversation with the present owner, I expressed puzzlement at the strange residential name – College Farm House. He went on to explain his own research into its history.

When Clarendon died, leaving large debts, the estate passed to his son Henry, who had his own debts. After a series of unpaid loans it was sold. In 1718, after another sale it came into the ownership of George Clarke, a highly educated and politically important member of society, who took the Degree Doctor of Civil Law and was intensely involved in Oxford University affairs. Because of his preoccupation in Worcester

Portrait of Edward Hyde by Jacob van Reesbroeck, 1649-1653

Mary II of England

College it was natural, on his demise, to leave all his property, including land in Purton, to the College. Hence the name College Farm and also College Road!

Another little anecdote of interest centres round the College Farm 'cheese door' now housed in the Museum. The window tax was a system of taxation used in the 17th and

18th centuries and was a property tax based on the number of windows in the house. Certain rooms, particularly dairies, cheese rooms and milk houses were exempt from this tax. College Farm House had one of these tax-avoidance rooms and then, as the window tax fell away, so the cheese room became redundant; the door disappeared and the room reinstated into the house. Now you know the story of the Cheese Door!

An old and well established family were the Maskelynes who held property in the Lydiards (an adjacent village) from as early as 1435 and later bought and owned land and homes in Purton itself. Many of their progeny distinguished themselves in various professions, but perhaps the

Nevil Maskelyne

most gifted was Nevil Maskelyne who became Astronomer Royal in 1756.

He began the publication of his Nautical Almanac which became his life-long pursuit. This innovative concept provided navigators with easy methods of determining longitude by lunar measurements at sea. Nevil is buried in the churchyard and his impressive tomb has recently undergone some conservation work and is now looking very smart.

What a small world – the famous Robert Clive was also connected to Purton! He married Maskelyne's sister Margaret.

The village of Purton was originally built around the parish church, manor and Tithe Barn. For some reason, which is uncertain, but possibly due to plague, it was to spread in a south westerly direction along what would later become the Bristol to Oxford Coaching Road.

The Manor House

The old Tithe Barn *(left)* stretches loftily along Church Road and, before the Dissolution, must have been a hive of activity.

The Church of England parish church of St Mary's is unusual in having a tower at the west end, and one at the centre which supports a spire. It is one of only three parish churches in England with both a spire and another tower.

Certainly in existence by the 12th century it sustained periods of rebuilding during the 13th, 14th and finally the 19th century. This last set of renovations currently serves the present congregation and was designed by the architect William Butterfield. It was at this time of the rebuilding that a woman's skeleton was found in a wall of the north transept. Mystery surrounds the discovery. Who was this lady and why was she contained within a wall? Unfortunately the finding could not be investigated to any great extent as the body fell away to dust on exposure to air.

But history moves on and the Church community is busy preparing for a whole new renewal programme which will, in a very short time, change the inside into a more comfortable and user-friendly sanctuary

Another intriguing story revolves around the theft of 'The Last Supper', *(pictured below)* painted by an artist of the school of Jacob Jordaens. This painting was presented to the church in 1782 as a gift from the Dowager Countess

of Shaftesbury. Along with two other paintings, 'The Last Supper' was stolen from the church in 1994 and suddenly appeared in the U.S. in 1998. After a complicated legal battle the painting, in a seriously damaged condition, was returned to the church. Restoration costs were estimated at £9,500 and the village rallied to an appeal for gifts and funding, much of which came in the form of grants. The painting has now resumed its rightful place above the altar with special lighting fitted to ensure that the splendour of its artistry is visible to all who frequent the church.

One final little snippet from the past is the Robert Watkins Story. Stephen Rodway, a merchant of Cricklade, was travelling home from Wootton Bassett when he was waylaid, robbed and shot by Robert Watkins on the night of 17 May 1819 close to the village of Purton Stoke. Incontrovertible evidence proved the guilt of Watkins. Edward, his brother, had buried the pistol, but was acquitted of the murder; Watkins was found guilty and sentenced to be hanged. A scaffold and gallows was erected at the site of the crime. A large crowd, in the region of well over 5000, collected to view the hanging.

THE
ROBERT WATKINS
STORY

Some 188 years after Watkins' death, the village of Purton Stoke relived Hang Fair Day – complete with mock murder, autopsy, trial and execution. Arkells, which owns the village pub, The Bell, concocted a special brew Gallows Ale ("a nice drop of ale"), while souvenir mugs were sold and a 44-page booklet was produced, *The Robert Watkins Story*.

Descendants of Watkins and Rodway gave their approval for the 2007 theatrical re-creation in aid of charity. Villagers in period costume re-enacted the drama – from judge, hangman and the condemned man to soldiers and spectators. One of the organisers, Denise Simpkins, said at the time: "It's an important though unfortunate part of our local history. People like me have been aware of it largely because of an old reproduced notice which has been displayed in The Bell for years."

Stephen Rodway had a grandson George Poulton who was born in Cricklade and baptised in St Mary's Church. At the age of seven his parents immigrated to New York. In 1861 George composed the song Aura Lee, one of the most popular songs of the 19th century and reached fame as an American Civil War song. In 1956 the song was given new lyrics and used by Elvis Presley as Love Me Tender. What a small world! A famous song - a famous singer – and all connected with Purton and Cricklade in Wiltshire.

Living in Purton for these last few years has been a joy. The villagers are warm, friendly and concerned. An incredible number of activities form part of village life and no one can ever complain of being bored or neglected. Two excellent schools ensure a fine education for the youth and proximity to Swindon enables the business man or woman to commute easily to the larger centres of Bristol and London. But although time ticks peacefully by for ordinary folk in Purton, visitors can be assured of a congenial and friendly welcome with much to see and plenty to enjoy.

CRICKLADE

Cricklade, the first town on the River Thames, is certainly a power house of historic information. It seems incredible that almost every building along the High Street has a momentous past all of its own.

Please note, that I have written 'town' not 'village'. To call Cricklade a village is a mark of some ignorance and definite disrespect. Besides confirmation gleaned from the annals of history, anyone who lives there will tell you, with great pride, that it has gained distinction as 'the most intact example of a late Saxon new town in England'.

One of my first visits to Cricklade was with a small group of visitors from the Purton Historical Society. We were off on a sunny, summer day's outing to enjoy a walking tour with John Samways, who would be our guide for the excursion.

His tour was interesting and informative and filled with personal observations and touches of humour.

We set out from the museum *(pictured left)*, which is a quaint little building rich in fascinating stories from the past. As a sanctuary, it progressed through a series of changes, from a Baptist Church in 1852 to a WVS canteen during WW2, then again, a place of worship, this time for the Roman Catholic Church, until it was leased in 1985 to the Cricklade Historical Society. Within its venerated walls it houses items dating over a period of almost 2000 years of local history. Viewing one of the showcases, I was intrigued by the display of Ockwell's gloves, which are reputed to have been of the very highest quality. I also learned that the original glove factory is now the council building *(right)*.

As we moved along Calcutt Street to begin our tour, John showed us one of the last surviving 'founding' stones - Meer Stones *(above)* - which is positioned on the boundary of Cricklade. The story told on the plaque is reproduced right.

MEER STONE

This Meer Stone is one of a number of stones that marked the boundary of Cricklade. It is the only one surviving and is cited in a 1776 parliamentary boundary dispute concerning the rights to vote of the occupiers of the properties comprising house numbers 17 to 23 Calcutt Street. The position of the Meer Stones is shown on an 18th century map of the Borough of Cricklade, which can be seen in the Cricklade Museum. This stone is also recorded in the Wiltshire Sites & Monument Records.

We ambled along a footpath to a ridge and furrow field dating from medieval times. In certain light conditions you can see evidence of the ploughing system which shows the ground having a corrugated effect.

We had a good look at the little Thames *(left)* adjacent to the field. How incredible to think that this gentle stream would wend its way through the countryside, gathering feeder tributaries along its meandering route, until it becomes the mighty Thames pouring its prodigious volume of water into the North Sea.

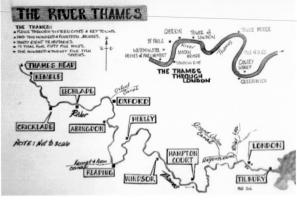

I found this map of the river route and it certainly travels a circuitous path as it wends its way eastward.

Eventually we moved along to Abingdon Court Farm which was built in the 17th century.

Abingdon Court manor *(below)* is recorded as having been created in 1008 by Aethelread II. In 2000 the farm became part of a smart modern housing complex. John informed us you had to be over 55 to live in this very stylish residential facility.

Although there had been earlier Iron Age trackways it was the Romans who built the first metalled road, Ermin Street, to cross the low flood plains between Speen and Gloucester.

The later walled Saxon town was built by Alfred the Great as a means of protection and defence against the Danes and was important enough to produce its own coinage system.

Most of the houses on the High Street still have their original allotted burgage plot length of 12 poles (198 feet) and frontage of 2 poles (33 feet) and, incredibly, people have lived on these plots for over 1000 years.

Opposite the council offices in the High Street is this most imposing Queen Anne house *(pictured right)*. It was once the home of a certain Morgan Byrt, a Bailiff who was involved in bribery and corruption at the parliamentary elections, and his fraudulent practices probably contributed to the presence of the rotten boroughs in the area. The term rotten borough is interesting; it came into use in the 18th century and was used to mean a parliamentary borough with a tiny electorate, so small that voters were susceptible to control and bribery in a variety of ways.

Cricklade High Street.

We were privileged to have access to the lovely Roman Catholic Church of St Mary's *(right)*, as John was able to procure the keys and give us a tour of this fascinating sanctuary. The Friends of St Mary's have published a beautifully illustrated and informative booklet describing the history of this ancient building as well as recording information of its remarkable features.

St Mary's has been a place of continuous Christian worship for over a thousand years and the impact of history is visible right through from Roman times into the 21st century.

The oldest item in the church is the font *(below left)* which was probably the top of a Roman pillar.

The Chancel Arch is the most striking feature of the church and the oldest part of the site is the curious North Chapel which stood on the line of the Saxon wall and could

possibly explain its mis-alignment with the rest of the church, seen above.

We had time for another peek at the baby Thames *(right)*, from the Town Bridge. The river seemed to have grown a little more in prestige during the last few hours.

There was so much more to see that we all split into groups to explore the town before meeting up for a welcome cup of coffee - or chilled beer - as the spirit so moved.

We ambled along the High Street, which has certainly changed in bustle and activity over the eons, but is definitely the same historic thoroughfare of character and distinction as it must have been a hundred and fifty years ago.

The Author with Ed on the Town Bridge

Just off the High Street is the famous Jenner Hall *(left)*. Robert Jenner, a Goldsmith in London, was the MP for Cricklade from 1628 to his death in 1651, and he had this school built for the boys in Cricklade. It is an example of one of the first free schools in England. As funds dwindled it served its purpose as the Parish Workhouse; but this closed and the inmates of the establishment later moved to a fine new building in Purton. Today the Jenner Hall opens its doors to all manner of activities - youth groups, art classes, bingo, choir, children's drama classes, toddlers' painting, belly dancing and it even functions as a parish office for St Sampson's church.

We went inside to have a look around and there are many signs of activity which show how well the church is patronised. In the churchyard I found an interesting snippet of information dating back to Victorian times. The Queen herself had forbidden any more graves to be sanctioned around the country and in the vicinity as it had become so overcrowded and, I expect, hazardous to health.

The Jubilee Clock *(right)* was erected in 1898 to celebrate Queen Victoria's Diamond Jubilee.

On a return visit to Cricklade Ed and I were walking along the busy High Street, when we popped into the local butcher's to buy some sausages. The staff were a cheerful, chatty group and I asked them if they enjoyed living and working in Cricklade. We were greeted with the usual answers of staff having job satisfaction, good working relations, ease of access to the work place! Suddenly we were joined by some of the customers who

The Jubilee Clock
photo Rick Dixon

St Sampson's church (left)
and graveyard (below)

joyfully sang praises of their Saxon town. They told us how friendly and supportive the community was and gave an example of a serious group of pub regulars who made it their business to raise funds for a needy charitable group; and they directed us to The Red Lion to see for ourselves.

Impressed by their enthusiasm I duly made my way to the 17th century pub and there, before my eyes, was

the famous corner table *(right)*, reserved in the evenings and weekends for a team of devotees. These staunch fund raisers merrily wiled away the social hours with the correct amount of lubrication and determined outreach to the public for their charitable support.

Showing vision and purpose this group of worthy citizens has been praised and thanked by the Wiltshire Air Ambulance with the presentation of a smart certificate. Well done to all!

The Red Lion
photo Rick Dixon

On the corner of High Street and North Wall, Bridge House *(left)* is the former home of Stephen Rodway, an established merchant of the town. He was the victim of the robbery and murder by Robert Watkins at Purton Stoke on 17 May 1819, described on page 11.

Ed and I enjoy the Victorian White Hart Hotel *(right)*. It is spacious and the staff friendly and helpful and, when league football is on view, it is a decidedly jolly venue!

Cricklade has become famous for its North Meadow Nature Reserve. The winter flooding in the area has nurtured the beautiful wild snake's head Fritillary bulbs, and about 500,000 emerge at the end of April and present a glorious feast of colour.

North Meadow is protected as a Special Area of Conservation and a Site of Special Scientific Interest. An old legend tells how the wild fritillary followed the path of the Romans and sprang up wherever they trod.

It was interesting to note the few existing glider blocks at the entrance of the meadow. These are all that remain of the hundreds which were spread across the area to prevent enemy gliders landing there.

North Meadow signage and a glider block

William Cobbett,
portrait in oils,
National Portrait Gallery, London

William Cobbett was a pamphleteer, farmer, journalist and member of parliament. He is famous for his activities in reforming the British Parliament especially regarding abolishing the "rotten boroughs". He would not have had much prior belief in democracy in Cricklade since with a tiny population it elected two Members to Parliament. His activities involved helping to end the farm labour poverty and the Corn Laws, which imposed a tax on imported grain. He became a radical and supported the Reform Act of 1832, which brought parliamentary seats more in line with the actual population size - and initiated a forerunner of the present Boundaries Commission. Though not a Catholic, he was one of the main players in allowing Catholicism to be openly practiced in Britain.

In 1821 Cobbett visited Cricklade. He was not impressed and couldn't wait to take his leave. He commented, *"I passed through that villainous hole, Cricklade, about two hours ago, and certainly a more rascally place I never set my eyes on. The labourers looked very poor, dwellings little better than pig beds and their food nearly equal to that of a pig."* Well William, if you could have taken a momentary peak into the future, I am sure you might wonder at the changes you helped bring about and form a new opinion. The distinctive Saxon Town today has a bright sparkle; it is neat, colourful and orderly.

It might seem appropriate that the Town motto today is *In loco delicto* - in a nice place!

You will so enjoy walking around this Saxon Town. It has several circular walking tours with walkers' guides and maps available from the Tourist Information desk at the Council Office. As you stroll along the well planned routes, myriad epochs of history will unfold and you will enjoy immeasurable delight in treading the chronicles of time.

Fritillaries among the primroses in North Meadow
(photo Helen Dixon, 2016)

Canal, Road & Rail

Cricklade isn't alone in Wiltshire in its connections to the outside world. An eight-mile section of canal called the North Wilts Canal opened in 1819 connecting the Wilts & Berks Canal into Swindon with the Thames & Severn Canal at Latton, just northwest of Cricklade. The canal in Cricklade had a wharf at Chelworth northeast of the town.

But then the railways arrived. The Midland and South Western Junction Railway (M&SWJR) linked the Midlands to the London & South Western Railway allowing a through route to the port of Southampton. Cricklade Station was part of that link, from Andoversford (near Cheltenham) and Cirencester, via Blunsdon (Purton) and Swindon (Old Town) through Savernake (Marlborough) and Andover (Hampshire) towards the south. With rail competition, a catastrophic canal viaduct collapse at Calne in 1901 wasn't economical to repair.

While the railways put the canal companies out of business, the railway companies fought it out between themselves. The M&SWJR was absorbed into its arch-enemy the Great Western Railway in the Railways (Grouping) Act of 1921 (into force in 1923).

Road travel became more accessible after the abolition of the toll roads (1857), improved road maintenance (1894), developments in motor vehicles and two World Wars. The Big Five companies were again in trouble before the Labour government in 1948 nationalised the railways in Britain. All the Wiltshire stations became part of the Western Region of British Railways. Road transport competition continued to pose a threat to the rail business despite simultaneous nationalisation of road transport. Even before the Beeching Report (1963, actioned by 1966) which closed many UK branch lines and stations, Cricklade and Blunsdon had already closed, and Purton in 1964.

The Swindon & Cricklade Railway runs a preserved steam and diesel route from its main station at Blunsdon, modified from a former milk-halt into a station, engineering works and visitor centre. The old tracks, ripped up in the 1960s, have been relaid north to Hayes Knoll Halt, (halfway from Blunsdon to Cricklade) and south to Mouldon Hill Country Park. A new station is in planning for Cricklade, but the site of the old station is now the Cricklade to Malmesbury Road (B4040) and the old goods yard is a housing area. The route to Swindon is also built upon and incorporates part of national cycle route 45.

Stations in towns and villages in this book are:

Purton, closed 1964
Cricklade, closed 1961, but Blunsdon Station (preserved section) Post Code SN25 2DA
Royal Wootton Bassett, closed 1965
Malmesbury, closed 1951
Lacock Halt, closed 1966
Devizes, closed 1966
Bradford-on-Avon (open: Avoncliff to Trowbridge
Chippenham (open: routes west from Paddington)
Marlborough (closed High Level 1933; Low Level 1966)
Salisbury (open: London Waterloo to Exeter)
Swindon (closed Old Town 1961; Mainline open: to Paddington, Bristol and West)
Highworth closed 1953

contributed by Rick Dixon

HISTORIC ROYAL WOOTTON BASSETT

Four miles from Purton is the North Wiltshire town of Royal Wootton Bassett. Early records document it as a Saxon holding 'Wodetun' in 681. In the Domesday Book of 1086 it was recorded as 'Wodetone' a possession of Milo Crispin. This settlement eventually came under the auspices of Alan Bassett, Lord of the Manor, in 1200. On 12 January 1219 King Henry III granted the little town the right to hold a weekly market and, through good times and bad, its fame and fortune have continued on this course right into the 21st century.

Photo courtesy of Royal Wootton Bassett Town Council

But Royal Wootton Bassett has not always been Royal. The change came about through the incredible spirit of sensitivity, care and compassion of the townsfolk who, as a whole community, acknowledged with respect the fallen soldiers as they moved in the slow hearse procession along the main street of the town during the Iraq and Afghanistan conflicts. The cortege columns were escorted through Wootton Bassett on their journey of repatriation from RAF Lyneham. The church bell tolled – work stopped – everyone moved out of shops or pubs and stood in silence with heads bowed. No one ordered, or suggested or urged their quiet presence. It was an affinity towards those who made the final sacrifice and a natural expression in honouring the bravery of young soldiers and sharing the grief of friends and family.

A beautiful memorial was positioned at the entrance of the town.

THE INSCRIPTION ALONGSIDE THIS POPPY READ

Forever
Unveiled by H R H the Princess Royal
and dedicated by
the Rt. Revd. the Bishop of Ramsbury
on 21st June 2016.

The stone poppy memorial was crafted from hard marble to represent the harshness of war; the white of the stone signified peace, illuminated by red in remembrance; its delicate petals showed the vulnerability of human life, shaped into four hearts to express gratitude, honour, love and respect; the petals met to form a cross as a symbol of sacrifice and forgiveness,

DONATED BY MARK HUMPHREY, CREATOR.

In a moving ceremony in March 2011, the Princess Royal, Princess Anne, on behalf of her Majesty the Queen, conferred on the town Royal Patronage to honour the support

and respect shown by the people for the servicemen and women who gave their lives in conflict. Wootton Bassett now became Royal Wootton Bassett and will remain so for all time. Sadly, this memorial was blown over in a freak storm and now awaits a decision on whether to repair it or replace it.

Jarra Brown was stationed at RAF Lyneham, a few miles west of Royal Wootton Bassett and he was in charge of the repatriation of British personnel killed in Iraq and Afghanistan. I watched a moving video clip on You Tube where he explained his heart-breaking experiences of those years until the station closed in 2012. He disclosed how he knew deeply each and every one of the 345 fallen servicemen he transported through Wootton Bassett. He was so saddened by the loss of these brave young people that he wrote a book '46 MILES' (which is the distance the hearses journeyed from RAF Lyneham to the John Radcliffe Infirmary mortuary in Oxford). He described that, having no scholastic tendencies, he set out to write a book, the execution of which became like a drug, taking long, intense hours and he frequently had to wipe away his tears as he worked. So Royal Wootton Bassett, you have certainly made your mark in history and will be remembered as having become the '...Epi-centre of National Grief'.

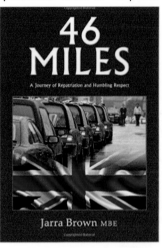

The town museum *(below)* dominates the High Street. It is a uniquely structured building which makes it a distinctive edifice amongst buildings of a much later era. Having been built as a town hall in about the 17th century, it was a gift of the Hyde Family. Edward

Hyde was the Earl of Clarendon *(mentioned in the Purton chapter).* In its early days the town hall had a slightly different appearance. Where the upper room or council chamber was used for the purpose of town

business, the lower level had a store room and a 'Blind House' for detaining drunks overnight. Legend has it that many drunks incarcerated late at night were even more drunk the following morning. This came about as a result of secret ministrations of 'midnight ale' that passed through the grating by means of the 'churchwarden pipe'. During some intensive restoration work initiated and supported by the wealthy Meux

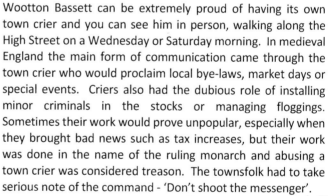

family, the Blind House disappeared. I am not sure what happened to the nightly drunks – they must have grown quite fond of their safe recluse after a night of heavy liquid consumption. The Museum is a fascinating place to visit and is open on Wednesday and Saturday mornings.

Diagonally opposite the Museum is a quaint little tea shop *(right)*. The smiling lady behind the counter assured me that it has its origins in the 13th century which makes it very old indeed. I am sure that its historic timbers have heard numerous whispered secrets and, could they but talk, would have many interesting tales to tell.

Wootton Bassett can be extremely proud of having its own town crier and you can see him in person, walking along the High Street on a Wednesday or Saturday morning. In medieval England the main form of communication came through the town crier who would proclaim local bye-laws, market days or special events. Criers also had the dubious role of installing minor criminals in the stocks or managing floggings. Sometimes their work would prove unpopular, especially when they brought bad news such as tax increases, but their work was done in the name of the ruling monarch and abusing a town crier was considered treason. The townsfolk had to take serious note of the command - 'Don't shoot the messenger'.

Although his work is now ceremonial, Owen Collier, the current town crier, takes the task very seriously. He might have to appear at local civic or national events, or help to promote charity functions. He might be asked to assist local businesses. He certainly adds an aura of panache as he colourfully blends in with the High Street shoppers furthering and promoting the important role of a market town.

And what a busy market town this is! Wednesday morning will have a display by local businesses. Once a month is Farmers' Market!

Delicious home baked tarts, biscuits and mouth-watering cakes!

Getting to know the work of the Wild Life Trust!

Spectacular Home Craft produce of Alfie Purl Yarns

I was intrigued by this market stall, which was called ALFIE PURL YARNS AND TEXTILES. It is owned by Emma, a lifelong knitter and hand spinner, and her husband Foz. They rear their own Cotswold sheep, which are their pets and are known by name. Their fleeces are sent to a small mill and processed into fibre or yarn. These are hand dyed in the most incredible colours by Emma and Foz and either sold as yarn or made into woven or knitted items. If you miss the Farmers' Market you can still do business with them on line.

Although there have been enormous changes, Wootton Bassett continues to be a warm, friendly, market town. It doesn't suffer from the chain store image and its greatest strength lies in the diversity and individualism of local trade – the hardware store, the butcher, the fabric and needlework store, an electrical store, the bookshop, several gift shops, the very necessary chemists and post office and numerous charity shops, which I frequently patronise.

This must be the crème-de-la-crème of all the little High Street shops *(right)*. It is a cornucopia of 19th century memorabilia and a real treasure trove of delight!

In The Pink

A delightful little flower shop!

And then there are the pubs. From very early days no market town would be without these very necessary establishments and Royal Wootton Bassett boasts more than an ample supply.

In looking at the Pub Reviews, the one that caught my attention was the Five Bells *(right)*. This quaint little pub with its thatched roof, beams and brick fireplace dates from the 1600s and its historical site indicates that it was very much part of the town community. Maybe some of their less-disciplined drinkers might have spent late nights in the Blind House. It is highly rated by visitors for its varied supply of ales, good food, friendly bar staff, clientele and warm environment.

The Angel *(left)* was in its time a traditional coaching inn and, now as a very central town inn, restaurant and pub; it has retained a great deal of old world charm and has delighted customers with home comforts, good food, friendly staff and historic ambience.

A major fire in 2013 halted the refurbishment of the Cross Keys, an old coaching inn. Enormous structural damage meant that flooring and roofing had to be replaced and strengthened to accommodate the fine new premises. Built in 1742, Cross Keys *(below)* is the oldest pub on the High Street and the unique and iconic building was a favourite meeting place for the townsfolk as well as serving as a sanctuary for many of the bereaved during the repatriation

services. I have had a peak into the newly refurbished establishment and I must say an excellent job has been done. Everything is shiny bright and new and the premises really looks most inviting.

Inside the Cross Keys

If you walk a short way along the High Street in the direction of Lyneham, you will come to the lovely old Parish Church of St Bartholomew and All Saints *(above right)*. The interior is peaceful, serene and well-appointed and the raised dais *(above left)* must lend itself admirably to congregation and parishioner involvement.

An earlier church was built in the 13th century by Fulk Bassett and many changes came about through the 14th and 15th centuries. Its position in the historic part of the town suggests that a small village grew up with the church as its focal point. Even now a pathway meanders through the graveyard from the High Street to the little cottages lying north of the church. Further changes in Victorian times have resulted in the lovely sanctuary the community enjoys today.

St Bartholomew has its own little coffee shop and Ed and I had a warming cup of cappuccino on a very cold morning. I was served by two delightful elderly ladies who informed me that they were both in their ninety's. I assured them that neither looked a day over eighty.

A really interesting historic building is Priory Cottage of No 28 Wood Street, not far from the church. In this vicinity was a small priory run by a priest and presbyters to feed 13 old men and was originally called the hospital of St John. Established by Sir Philip Bassett in 1254, it only survived until the 1400s. The present cottage is about 300 years old and I am told by the town crier it has its own ghost. A shrouded monk walks quietly through the walls of bedrooms to bend down and feel the artery in the neck of the sleeper checking for signs of life. If you encounter him just roll over and sleep on – he is perfectly

Priory Cottage

harmless. But the cottage has another claim to fame. It was owned by Brig. Gen J H Morgan who was a Professor of Constitutional Law, Deputy Adjutant General at the Inter Allied Military Commission of Control in Berlin 1919 to 1923 and legal adviser to the War Crimes Commission Nuremburg 1947 to 1949. He is buried in Wootton Bassett cemetery.

The historic building which most captures the imagination is Vastern Manor House *(below)*. Along the top of the ridge, the High Street runs for nearly a mile. Just south west of the town the ridge narrows and dips and on the high ground beyond this Gilbert Bassett built his great house of Vastern in the 13th century. The large establishment

encompassed a brew house, bake house, kitchen, barns and fish ponds. Various changes of ownership took place over the years and, sadly, the house suffered periods of neglect and fell into disrepair. In the 1500s the manor of Wootton, including the borough of Wootton and the park of Vastern formed part of the jointure of the Queens of England. And so it became a livelihood of freehold for Katharine of Aragon, Anne of Cleves, Katharine Howard

and finally Katherine Parr. The lavishness of royal households must have brightened and enriched the house and one need only visualise sumptuous dining and elite gatherings to

conjecture on the historical pageant. But with the demise of Katherine Parr tenure changed. Gifts were made to nobles who fell in and out of favour; sometimes purchasers took possession of the property; so Vastern Manor passed from one owner to the next and, bereft of love and care, time took its toll. When James Waylen, a historian, visited the house in 1849 he commented that it was 'but a shadow of its former self'. It took the riches and affluence of the wealthy Meux family to help restore Vastern Manor House to a vestige of its former glory.

The house is now a private residence but, if you are visiting the golf club over the motorway and happen to be waiting for your opponent to reach the green, pause a while. Look across the road at the famous old building, an embodiment of the chronicles of passing time, and envisage the pageant of history that once moved along that sumptuous drive way.

The railway line from London to Bristol was constructed through the parish and a station, Wootton Bassett Junction, was launched with a new main railway line to South Wales opened in 1903. The Dairy Supply Company positioned its factories near the station in 1908 and milk was transported to the London market. Sadly, with a parliamentary restructuring of railway, Wootton Bassett was closed in 1966,

Royal Wootton Bassett has its own Rugby Club, the Lime Kiln Sports Centre which offers a varied choice of sports and activities, a range of carnivals and festivals throughout the year, Infants, Primary and Secondary Schools, a well-stocked library, a Community Cinema, a Light Operatic Society and theatre group and a wonderful Christmas Lights and Shopping Event which takes place in the High Street on the first Friday of December each year. For nature lovers and wildlife enthusiasts there is the spectacular Jubilee Lake. With all this on offer, Royal Wootton Bassett is not only a historic market town but a vibrant, active and inspirational community which will certainly offer the visitor a great many pastimes to appreciate and enjoy.

MALMESBURY

Although Malmesbury is noted to be the oldest Borough in England, there is also a great deal of evidence of very early settlement linking the Stone Age, Iron Age and Roman occupation right through to the Dark Ages. Through time it grew in importance and was certainly well defended with its position at the top of a hill and almost encircled by the River Avon.

Malmesbury Town Hall which houses the Athelstan Museum

A Benedictine monk deep in meditation:
> *Oh, what can ail thee silent monk*
> *Alone and paling musing*
> *The heather's withered from the hearth*
> *And no bird sings.*
> *My thoughts are on eternal cares*
> *Of mankind's woes, of hurts and fears,*
> *Oh God, I pray you lift this yoke*
> *And wipe away the pain and tears.*

[Mostly my words but inspired by Keats and the Silent Monk.]

Although the Benedictine Monk has only been in his state of soliloquy and solitude *(above)* since 2014, his presence is timeless and the deep weight of worldly discord and suffering hangs heavy on his brooding shoulders.

The statue was one of my first encounters with Malmesbury and I was deeply enamoured of the monk's self-effacing and passive acceptance of his legacy and role in spiritual life. But his sadness left me with a strange depression. I hoped that on my next visit circumstances would have made him more content and perhaps he would even have been able to smile a little.

The statue of the Benedictine monk is a fitting reminder of the integral role that monks played in shaping the very character of the historic town that we know today. One of the most notable of these was the Irish monk Maildub. He set up a hermitage and soon had a collection of students, one of whom was Aldhelm, the renowned scholar who, after travelling widely in Europe, returned and established a monastery in 676 AD.

Aldhelm was an amazing scholar. He was fluent in Latin and Greek and could read the Hebrew Old Testament. He wrote poetry, composed music and sang. He was a gifted musician skilled at playing different instruments including the harp, fiddle and pipes. He built the first church organ in Britain – 'a mighty instrument with innumerable tones and blown with bellows'.

And yet he was also intent on establishing a vigorous Christian community. Apart from his attachment to Malmesbury, he later became Bishop of Sherborne. However, the story which impressed me most about this saintly man was his concern over

inattentive and unfocused parishioners at religious services. So he stationed himself on a bridge and began to sing his ballads. After drawing a large crowd, who were greatly appreciative of his verse, he gained their attention and started to preach the gospel. Was he the Medieval equivalent of a Goethe, da Vinci or Erasmus? We will never know, but his fame pursued him well into the 12th century when his verse was still familiar and enjoyed by many.

A stained-glass window in the Catholic Church of St Aldhelm, Malmesbury, dedicated to the Saint.

After his death in 709, Aldhelm was canonised, and Malmesbury became a centre of pilgrimage.

Built in the 12th century, the Abbey *(right)* is certainly the most important and celebrated historic attraction of Malmesbury, and draws countless tourists to its hallowed halls all through the year. Although imposing it is only a shell of its original magnificent structure.

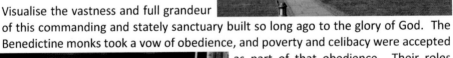

Visualise the vastness and full grandeur of this commanding and stately sanctuary built so long ago to the glory of God. The Benedictine monks took a vow of obedience, and poverty and celibacy were accepted

as part of that obedience. Their roles were to feed the hungry, heal the sick, provide education, copy manuscripts and preserve valuable books.

The Bible in Malmesbury Abbey written in Belgium in 1407 AD and used for reading aloud in the monastery.

A visualisation of how the Abbey might have looked in its heyday.

Aldhelm was naturally the most famous of these monks and it is mentioned how he chastised his own body by bathing in the Avon during the cold winter months. Sadly, not all monks lived to the same high standard and in 1527 the Abbot of Gloucester visited Malmesbury Abbey and was informed of poor leadership, neglect and disorder and the complete failure of living within holy orders under the leadership of Abbot Camme. He promptly excommunicated six monks and set about re-establishing strict Benedictine rule, starting with the wayward Abbot Camme himself.

Another famous monk who captures the imagination was Eilmer, the flying monk.

Procuring this photo was no easy feat. It is only clearly visible in a little side room with a half door. The church attendant kindly unlocked this door and invited me to take the necessary photo. He insisted on bringing in a very tall ladder which he helped me to ascend so that I could be at eye level with the window. Mounting the first few steps was fine but the nearer I got to the top the more my legs began to wobble. Then at the very top I started to laugh at my ridiculous situation. I couldn't find firm footing and negotiating a focused camera shot was now, not only complex, but hazardous. However, I managed to capture the image of Eilmer. The assistant was happy – and I was delighted to be back on terra firma.

The picture shows Eilmer holding a pair of wings which represent his attempt at achieving his concept of flight. He was a noted astrologer and was obviously much taken by the story of Daedalus. So, with man-made wings strapped to his feet and hands he flung himself from the abbey tower and attempted to negotiate

Permission to use this picture of Eilmer has been granted by Malmesbury Abbey.

currents of air in an aeronautical enterprise. Not being as adept as a bird in flight he quickly found himself plunging to earth and ended up still alive but with 2 broken legs.

However, he had negotiated 200 metres successfully. The abbot banned him from any further attempts.

When Edward the Confessor had a disturbing dream, it was interpreted by two monks as a vision of an impending invasion of his kingdom because of the sins of earls, bishops, abbots and those in holy orders. The prophecy played out in the Norman invasions after which William of Malmesbury *(pictured right)* wrote -

We have experienced the truth of this prophecy, for England has become the habitation of outsiders and the dominion of foreigners. Today, no Englishman is earl, bishop, or abbot, and newcomers gnaw away at the riches and very innards of England; nor is there any hope for an end of this misery.

With a never-ending migration into the UK is this prophecy still applicable today? William spent his whole life as a monk and librarian in Malmesbury Abbey. He is recognised as the foremost English Historian of the 12th century with his most famous work being The Deeds of the Kings of England, and under his care the library became famous. Sadly, after his death, this noble institution declined and many books were lost; the Athelstan Museum tells a story of how the vellum pages of ancient writings were used as stoppers for beer barrels.

Besides the Abbey, there are many more interesting attractions to enjoy.

The Old Bell *(left)*, which is now a Grade 1 listed building, lays claim to being the oldest hotel in England. It served originally as a guest house for Abbey visitors and today has been transformed into luxurious tourist accommodation. Some years ago, Ed and I used their comfortable lounge to order a cup of coffee. It was beautifully and tastefully served by a smartly dressed waiter – but it was the worst cup of coffee we have ever tasted. Their catering facilities, however, have shown an enormous improvement and on many ensuing visits I have enjoyed delicious lunches with hot and cold beverages. The Old Bell can certainly boast of its very own ghost, the Grey Lady, whose melancholy visage has been seen by visitors and staff alike. She tends to haunt the James Ody room, housed on the east side of the hotel, a section which was built on part of the former abbey churchyard. Poor lady, here's hoping she finds what she is looking for on her nightly travels.

This statue *(left)* at the entrance to the Abbey Gardens assures visitors that if they want to take their clothes off they are welcome to do so. In fine weather, the previous owners, Ian and Barbara Pollard, did all their gardening in the 'all-together'! It is a magnificent garden full of manicured wandering paths as well as a lower section which descends down to the Avon. Here you will cross the line of the town's ancient Saxon defences and encounter the monastic fishponds and St Aldhelm's pool. The incredible bird song from the many feathered occupants and the gentle sound of the river meandering slowly by, transports one into an unspoiled world of enchantment. If you have time, watch the BBC iPlayer Country File on the Abbey Gardens.

The Beautiful Abbey Gardens

The Market Cross dating back to 1490.

The Whole Hog – a warm and friendly pub with good beer for me and good coffee for patient Ed!

The busy High Street which descends steeply down to the River Avon! I completed the descent and ascent in about half an hour – charming but tiring.

*The River Avon flowing
merrily along.*

Part of the Friday market in the Village Square. I was informed that market trading only becomes intense as the summer season progresses.

Malmesbury's history as a market town can be traced back to 927 when King Athelstan *(pictured right)*, King Alfred's grandson, ruled England.

Life was far from easy during the Dark Ages and England sustained continual raids from the Danes. It was not until the time of King Athelstan that the Saxons were able to push the Danes back north.

Athelstan was possibly one of the greatest English kings; he was attached to the Abbey and a great admirer of the revered St Aldhelm. He unified the country, brought peace to the land, instituted many new laws, reformed the currency, bestowed a charter

*Athelstan
'King of All England'*

on the town permitting it to hold a market and be exempt from certain taxes and gave many gifts to the abbey, which allowed it to grow in wealth and importance.

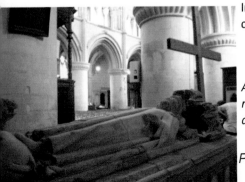

In 1180 the great Abbey was finally consecrated; it featured a spire taller than that

Athelstan's tomb is in the abbey but his remains lie buried somewhere in the abbey grounds.

Page 34

of Salisbury Cathedral. The 12th century saw struggles between Stephen and Matilda and final combat between Stephen and Henry, who was later to become Henry II. The dissolution of the monasteries saw a new era of change for Malmesbury. Fortunately for the market town a merchant, William Stumpe purchased the abbey lands and, although he used much of the building for his wool, cloth and looms he gave the nave to the town to be used as a parish church.

Thomas Hobbes

In Fifteen hundred eighty eight, old style,
When the Armada did invade our isle,
Call'd the Invincible; whose Freight was then,
Nothing but Murd'ring Steel and Murd'ring Men;
Most of which Navy was disperst, or lost,
And had the Fate to Perish on our Coast:
April the fifth (though now with Age outworn)
I'th'early Spring, I, a poor worm, was born.
In Malmesbury Baptiz'd, and Named there
By my own Father, then a Minister.

Thomas Hobbes

Thomas Hobbes was born in Malmesbury. He was educated here and at the age of 14 went to Oxford. He was an esteemed writer and philosopher and is famous for his book, Leviathan, which takes its name from the biblical Leviathan and focuses on his beliefs concerning the structure of society and legitimate government.

Malmesbury, sited in a strategic position between Oxford and Bristol, could not escape the civil war and changed hands between Cavaliers and Roundheads six times. Eventually, after enduring siege after siege Malmesbury was spared further involvement and came to enjoy a period of relative peace and calm.

This grave stone of Hannah Twynnoy *(left)* can be found in the Abbey grounds. Aged

33, she became the first person to be killed by a tiger in Britain. She was employed locally as a waitress but met her fate in goading a tiger which escaped from a menagerie. Sadly, her taunting resulted in the tiger's attack and her death.

WIKIPEDIA assures us that, although an ill-fated waitress, the town has not forgotten her sad demise. A new residential road in Malmesbury has been named Twynnoy Close. Furthermore, to commemorate the 300th anniversary of her death, a modest ceremony was held where every schoolgirl under the age of 11 and named Hannah bequeathed a flower to her grave.

My final chronicle of interesting Malmesbury personalities deals with Walter Powell, the Member of Parliament for Malmesbury in 1869. He was popular, rich and generous. But he is remembered most for his hobby as a balloonist.

In December 1881 Walter Powell flew his balloon, Saladin, with two friends to take some meteorological observations. The balloon got into difficulties and they managed to land on a beach. The two friends hastily clambered out, one breaking his leg, and some of the ballast was removed. Now, being lighter, the balloon took off with only Walter on board. It flew majestically out to sea and was never seen again.

The balloon Eclipse about to take off from Cross Hayes, Malmesbury

Exploring Malmesbury has given me enormous pleasure. I have loved the old world charm of the town with its fascinating High Street, beguiling shops offering merchandise to satisfy any tourist, the history of the buildings and abbey, the comfort of pubs and restaurants, the beauty of the gardens and the wonderful people who walked through Malmesbury's pages of history.

Visit Malmesbury – you won't be disappointed.

CASTLE COOMBE
The Prettiest Village in England

It was a lovely June morning when Ed and I set out to explore Castle Combe. This was not our first visit; we had been twice before during the colder months. So, this was a new sunny experience! Imagine my delight, en route, to drive through a tiny village of eight houses called Tiddlywink.

I half expected Big Ears and Noddy to pop out through one of the closeted little dwellings and rush off on a new adventure. But perhaps they were too busy inside planning a party with all their special friends!

It didn't take us long to find parking in Castle Combe and amble down the steep incline to this quaint little village. In recent times, Castle Combe has boasted a population of 350 residents, and, with tourist traffic, this number is often doubled.

I had heard about Castle Combe from many acquaintances and often read interesting accounts relating to the village. But on previous visits I had never found the castle. I engaged in conversation with a resident of the village and asked –

"Excuse me, could you please show me where the castle is?"

"Oh, no my dear, there is no castle," was the reply.

"Then how do you explain the village name?" I asked.

"Ah, well, that's a long story…"

Like all the wonderful tales from the past, it is a long story – and this is what I found out.

A Saxon entrenched camp, which had been destroyed by the Danes, was possibly the site of a motte and bailey when Reginald de Dunstanville became the first Baron and is

A villager's cottage

credited with building a castle in 1140 AD. The castle then became the feudal seat of the Barony. As time passed and peace prevailed, defence was no longer the

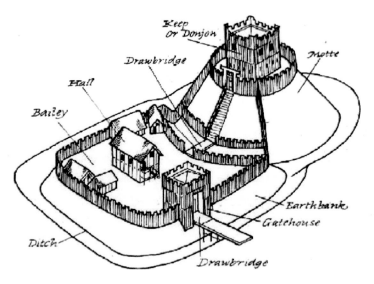

The Castle as it my have looked in Saxon times.

demanding issue that it had been, and a more convenient and comfortable house was built on the valley floor in the 14th century. The castle fell into disrepair and, apart from heavily covered earthenware remnants, is no longer visible to the tourist and lies concealed under encroaching shrubbery in a private golf course area.

So, there **WAS** a castle ... although only a minor and ancient one! And the village has a genuine claim to its name!

Castle Combe is situated in a conservation area just south of the Cotswolds and has earned the reputation of being the prettiest village in England.

By the Middle Ages the village prospered as an important centre for the wool industry and weekly markets were a valuable source of revenue.

Sheep by the Market Cross
[Photo taken c. 1905. Courtesy of Wiltshire & Swindon History Centre, Chippenham]

The village street

As I walked along its charming streets I was moved by the tranquillity and stillness; only the gentle murmur of the fluid river and the cadence of twittering birds stirred the consciousness. It was a glorious moment of unspoiled magic in this timeless village.

The streets are lined with aged limestone cottages, which were erected for the weavers of the village. Each breathes its own fragrance of history.

The Dower House *(right)* is a Grade II

listed building and stands out a little solemnly from the other more picturesque cottages along the road. This was used as Dr Dolittle's house when filming started for the movie in 1967.

There is a quaint little tea and gift shop along the way. If you ring the bell you will be invited to enter, either to make purchases or to indulge in a specially prepared afternoon

tea. The owner is friendly and graciously showed me her souvenir book of War Horse, which was filmed in the village.

The Old Rectory

The Market Cross dating to the 14th century

THE GARDEN OF REMEMBRANCE

Beautifully appointed, this little garden is tucked into a sheltered nook close to the church. Amazing to think that, even in this small village, there were those who gave their lives as the final sacrifice in two world wars.

The lovely old St Andrew's Church *(left)* had its origins in the 13th century but over time sections were added and in 1850 renovation and rebuilding became imperative as much of the church fell into disrepair.

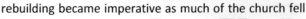

I walked into the graveyard and was amazed to see how extensively it spread around the church, even descending into a large, densely occupied lower level. It was reminiscent of Thornton Wilder's 'Our Town' and I wondered if Castle Combe, in any way, resembled Grover's Corners; or if, like Emily, anyone had made the painful venture back to earth. Perhaps those who sat beside their gravestones warned that it was foolish to return.

The church has a beautiful interior and all looks so orderly and calm that any roof deterioration problems are obscured. To address their repair challenges, St Andrew's has launched an impressive fund-raising campaign.

They have procured the rights from DreamWorks Pictures to display photographs of the recent film, War Horse, which was filmed in the village.

Photographs clockwise from top left:

St Andrew's exterior

The Garden of Remembrance

The Graveyard

St Andrew's aisle looking towards the chancel

War Horse – filmed in Castle Combe

What an enterprising idea and how generous of DreamWorks to facilitate the renovation process of St Andrews. I photographed some of the exhibition and duly donated a small sum towards the roof repair appeal.

There are other interesting exhibits in the church.

In the Lady Chapel is a splendid monument of Sir Walter de Dunstanville *(left)* who was Baron of Castle Combe before he died in 1270. His crossed legs show that, in his years of combat, he was a participant in two crusades.

The arms of the Scrope family are visible above the tomb.

The unusual crucifix *(right)* commands a strategic position in the church and invites the visitor to pause in respect and reflection.

This famous medieval clock is faceless and strikes a bell in the church tower. It is thought to have been made by a locksmith and is amongst the oldest working clocks in England.

Leaving the fascinating church, I wondered back to the Market Cross where two famous pubs stand harmoniously close to each other.

The medieval clock mechanism

Wonderful Wiltshire

The Castle Inn *(right)* dates back to the 12th century and has all the old-world charm you would expect to find in this fascinating little village. We had a quick peek inside and it is beautifully appointed with comfortable seating and agreeable entertainment areas, plus the outside catering for those who want to soak up the sun. It appears that, at one time, the Inn was a favourite retreat of Oliver Cromwell.

The White Hart

While I was wandering around the village Ed ensconced himself comfortably in the White Hart and refreshed himself with a generous helping of coffee. When I joined him later, we decided to have lunch in the unusual form of 'doorstep sandwiches', which would naturally be washed down with some chilled draught lager. I couldn't believe what arrived at our table – sausage sandwich for Ed and hearty ploughman's for me. Absolutely superb!

My sandwiches were so overflowing with ploughman's fare that they bulged invitingly with their wonderful fillings, and chunky onion chutney oozed from every corner. The seeded, wholegrain bread was soft and tasty. No wonder a knife and fork are provided to tackle the meal.

Ed couldn't believe the tastiness of his sausage sandwich which was smothered in onions 'just the way he likes them'. Of course, neither of us could finish our generous meal, but it was great fun trying.

Ed and lunch!

We returned the following week to visit the Manor House with a reservation for Afternoon Tea. Both of us were curious to find out whether they could offer the same tasty indulgence we had enjoyed at the White Hart.

It was a pricey, little banquet, but well worth the outing. Ed and I devoured almost every sandwich, cream scone and elegant cupcake on our tiered cake stand. The Manor House calls it - *"Ultimate luxury... A decadent, home-made afternoon tea for two (or more) served on a tiered cake stand with a glamorous sense of tradition and occasion."* We were certainly well pampered by a host of charming staff.

The Manor House *(left)* is a superb 14th century building positioned in 365 acres of beautiful parkland. It was built to replace the Norman castle which had fallen into a state of disrepair. There were many Lords of the manor who were to grace its noble hall, but the one that is best remembered is Sir john Falstaff, an English knight during the Hundred Years Wars. He became, perhaps not true to nature and disposition, the prototype for Shakespeare's comic character in Henry IV.

The Scrope family held the manor of Combe for almost 500 years. Remembered for his research of Castle Combe's Barony in 1852 is George Poullet Thompson, who took the family name on his marriage to Emma Scrope heiress to the Castle Combe estate.

George Scrope was an esteemed economist, politician and geologist. Articulate, and an accomplished writer, he effectively made his views known and, after years fulfilling the role of a magistrate, when he was affected with the hardships of agricultural labour, he eventually gained a seat in Parliament.

Emma had suffered a riding accident and was unable to bear children. I found it interesting that, like the way of the flesh, George retained a mistress who was comfortably established in London. She produced a son whom they called Arthur Hamilton. George ensured that he had the best education at Eton and Oxford and later he and Emma adopted Arthur. Even more interesting – when Emma died George married again to

George Julius Poulet Scrope – Encyclopaedia Britannica. Engraving of 1875

Margaret Elizabeth Savage – 44 years his junior!!! Naturally, his young wife and son survived him.

Scrope left behind important historical documentation about Castle Combe when he wrote and published his book The History of Castle Combe 1852. He died in 1876.

In 1947 the manor house was sold and, under new owners, soon emerged as a beautiful country hotel. It has a Championship Golf Course in idyllic settings, Italian Gardens and manicured lawns which cascade down to the River Bybrook.

The Roman Bridge *(left)* can be found at the end of the village. There is a legend that the ghost of a Roman soldier keeps faith in his arduous task of guarding the once military site.

The village is surrounded by dense woods and from time to time battle sounds of fighting men can be heard echoing through the dense growth, as swords clash and warriors cry out in ferocious combat. Who knows what ancient hordes, lost in the mists of time, faced each other in these sheltered and benign groves?

Legend further tells us that, within the Manor House, a Grey Lady drifts peacefully through the halls, unobtrusive and serene. Her haunting might derive from Norman times where the castle preceded the manor house.

The village possesses a racetrack which was the site of a former world war two airfield. Much of the village fame comes through its picturesque quality and being a superb location as a site for films and television production. It has been used to screen movies and series such as Dr Dolitte, Poirot, Stardust, The Wolfman, Downton Abbey and, perhaps most famous of all, War Horse.

If you are fortunate enough to make a visit to this charming village, you will remember it with fondness for many years to come.

Woods above the bridge

LACOCK ABBEY

Lacock Abbey and Lacock village are so steeped in history that one is overwhelmed with the magnitude of events which tumble from the pages of the past. It is an abbey which has been taken over by the National Trust, and is frequented by countless

visitors, some to see its origins under the first abbess, some to view the Talbot magic and some to walk in the footsteps of Harry Potter, but all with a great expectancy of sharing in a long-forgotten era.

But let's begin at the beginning.

One of the most important features in Lacock is the abbey and the origins of this wonderful building are the inspiration

of that incredible lady Ela, Countess of Salisbury. She seems to have been a woman full of endless energies and virtues.

Her early life is a little unclear, but an arranged marriage was her destiny.   She and William Longespee, the illegitimate son of Henry II, were married, and their lives

Top: Lacock Abbey under brooding clouds

Centre: The bell metal cauldron in the Warming Room

Right the cloister

progressed into a short but happy and fulfilling period. William took his father-in-law's title and became the Earl of Salisbury and Sheriff of Wiltshire. Ela and William contributed to laying the foundation stones of the mighty Salisbury Cathedral. It was here that William was buried *(right)*, and it was here that their youngest son Nicholas was to become Bishop of Salisbury.

Ela was devoted to her husband and, from all accounts, their marriage was a happy one. When he died Ela was left with eight children, four boys and four girls. William Longespee II, the eldest of the children, acquitted himself with great valour in the Crusades.

It was during the Seventh Crusade that he was lured into attacking the Mamelukes by Count d'Artois before French support had arrived. He chose rather to die fighting for Christ as an honourable crusader than to yield to the Saracens and he and his men, 280 Knights Templar, were killed in battle. His acts of chivalry and his martyrdom were remembered with pride by those he left behind and there is an effigy of him in Salisbury Cathedral *(right)*. I visited this in the Cathedral where there seems to be some doubt to the dating of this effigy. Nevertheless it certainly commemorates that wonderful young man.

Ella was grief-stricken with the death of her husband and went into a period of deep mourning. She founded the religious order at Lacock in 1229, finally entering the abbey herself as a nun and later becoming the abbess.

'Annals and Antiquities of Lacock Abbey' by Bowles and Nicholls is an incredible collection of historical narrative and data and gives a fascinating description of life in the abbey. The nuns endured a life of total obedience and constant prayer at appointed hours. 'They were to overcome their flesh with fasting and abstinence.' They had beds of straw with one or two blankets. There was a strict rule of silence and it was permitted for no one to leave the abbey's cloisters once they had been admitted. With constant prayer and devotion to duty the boundaries of earth and heaven must slowly have merged until life transfused into an ethereal periphery. The lines of the Poet of Paraclete from the Bowles and Nicholls book are melancholy.

How happy is the blameless Vestal's lot,
The world forgetting, by the world forgot,
Labour and rest that equal periods keep
Obedient slumbers than can wake or sleep
Desires composed, affections ever even
Tears that delight and sighs that waft to Heaven.

Was this how Ela chose to deal with her grief so that 'souls separated by Death' might be united in the contemplation of fervent piety?

However Ela was a woman of great strength and enterprise and was able to overcome her anguish. She worked tirelessly to ensure that the abbey and village earned certain rights and privileges and that it should flourish with local trade and markets. She ceased being the abbess before her death but still remained in the convent. Her funeral was one of great state and honour and her tomb, which was moved from the church, now lies in the cloisters.

With the dissolution of the monasteries Lacock Abbey was bought by William Sharington. He closed the abbey church and converted the house into a splendid home for himself.

In 1546 he became the 'under-treasurer' at the mint at Bristol Castle. Unfortunately, he abused his position, involving himself in fraudulent practices with misappropriation of the coins and embezzlement. This led him to a liaison with Thomas Seymour who was conspiring to overthrow the government of his brother Edward Seymour and capture the boy king Edward VI.

The plot was discovered and both men were imprisoned in The Tower. Thomas was beheaded but somehow William, by blaming his erstwhile conspirator and with the help of influential friends, managed a royal pardon. He had lost lands and prominence but, over time, retrieved some measure of his former prestige.

A picture of
Sharington by Holbein

How interesting to see the fate of William interwoven with the illustrious Seymour family from Savernake Forest in Marlborough – but then, how far is Marlborough from Lacock? According to the website it is a matter of 35 miles; so activities in Wiltshire were bound to be tangled and compromised, especially when persons of high degree were focusing on furthering their own interests.

William Henry Fox Talbot became the owner of the abbey in the 1800s. He was a renowned mathematician, astronomer and archaeologist; a very worthy gentleman whose claim to fame came through his experiments with photography when he produced a photographic camera negative of a window image.

There is a special museum at the abbey which is dedicated to his work, together with a collection of historical photographs. These show that his ideas were far more advanced than other scientists who were working on similar projects at the time. His 'calotype' process was patented in 1841 and brought another aspect of importance to the little village of Lacock.

The house and village were given to the National Trust in 1944 and over this period of time it has developed into a

William Henry Fox Talbot

vital tourist attraction. Lacock certainly is a village of extraordinary charm. The visitor might be forgiven for being transported into another time cosmos, another mystical cycle of a long-forgotten past.

The only intrusion to the setting is the visual impact of the enthusiastic tourist. The present day is barely visible – no overhead wires – no television aerials – no little white traders' vans – no shopping hypermarkets. The golden cottages nestle peacefully into their time-honoured sanctuaries. If you close your eyes to the diversions and breathe in history, you can feel the pulse of the chronicles of time; you can be one with the thousands who walked before you on these very roads and paths. If you listen well you can hear the clamour of their voices and each has his own story to tell.

From Saxon and Norman times through to the Middle Ages, the civil wars, restoration, 18th and 19th centuries, Lacock had fared well in its market industries and as a farming community.

History continues as new players take the stage. Today, leasing the houses has become an important part of the

Lacock's War Memorial

Trust's programme and a little school still operates right here in historical Lacock. I watched some of the children at play and they looked so much at home – all filled with youthful energy and joy.

St Cyriac's church *(left)* is a pivotal point in the village. Of Norman origins it was added to until it reached its towering splendour in the 15th century. St Cyriac is a saint who was popular with the Normans. He was martyred as a Christian during Diocletian's persecutions.

As Lacock was a prosperous market town, raising funds for the necessary improvements was not an onerous task and the result was a church in the popular perpendicular style which was so much part of English architecture at the time.

The church has many commemorative icons to celebrate important persons from the village.

The tomb on the left belongs to Sharington and is particularly impressive. Obviously his clandestine operations with the Bristol Mint produced sufficient funds to ensure a stately departure.

St Cyriac's chancel

Wikipedia gives an interesting account of the Medieval Silver Chalice which was known as the Lacock Cup. It dates from the 15th century and earned distinction as 'one of the most significant pieces of secular English medieval silver'.

In 2009 the cup was valued at £1.8 million! Imagine that valuable item lying around the nave or the vestry, with doors unlocked and visitors welcomed in, as is the custom in English churches!

It was sold in 2012 where both the British and the Wiltshire Museums placed a bid for ownership. Funds from the sale are channelled into restoration of the church and two replicas will be made of the cup, one for liturgical use and one for display in the Wiltshire Museum when the original is on display in the British Museum.

The National Trust has an excellent Restaurant where the tea-time treats are all freshly prepared and really good value for money.

There are several delightful shops in the village all selling either craft work, innovative confectionery, stationery or memorabilia to take home as a keepsake after an illuminating visit. I particularly enjoyed platform 9 ¾ at the Hogwart's Express *(right)*.

The Red Lion *(left)* is a lovely old pub with timbered ceilings, a delightful outside garden and an excellent menu.

The George Inn *(below)* has all the old-world charm you would expect to see in this historic village. Customer reviews are all very positive and visitors have enjoyed the good service and ambience. I took a peek at the Christmas menu – my word but it is tempting and the two-course meal is easily affordable.

I asked two of the local residents where they would choose to eat in Lacock and both unequivocally chorused, 'Sign of the Angel!' So that is where we went for a late lunch.

Standing in its heavy framed timbered door-way allows one an experience of historical fantasy. In the right attire one would be enjoying the pleasure of a vintage moment. It is quite delightful that the sign outside advertises the premises with a resident ghost. From what I have read she is a lady ghost who is friendly and well-mannered and probably delights in guests enjoying the fine fare at her inn.

The black and white timbered 15th century building *(right)* was once a wool merchant's house. Now it occupies pride of place as a well-patronised inn.

To enter the restaurant area you traverse a narrow passage and then turn to the right through a rustic doorway.

The restaurant is full of old-world charm and boasts huge open fire places which, on an autumn day, were lit with scattered candles, but must be glorious in the winter with cheerful, crackling fires. It splits into two areas and we were shown into the second room to a cosy little table tucked away in a corner. I have read several customer reviews about the diverse food selection and all have been glowing – and here I must add my praises for a culinary delight I had not expected would be so pleasurable.

While we made our menu selections a little platter of bread, cheese and oil appeared. How civilized I thought, delighted with a treat which is above and beyond your normal pub fair.

Ed selected a haddock and poached egg muffin with spinach and champagne cream, while I had tiger prawn tagliatelle with courgette, tomato, spinach and lobster sauce. Now, having worked in school and hotel catering for many years, I pride myself on the ability to identify the ingredients in any particular dish, but today I was at a loss. The prawns were sautéed to perfection and the sauce had a piquant, savoury texture which

was superb. I knew I wouldn't be able to copy this tantalizing dish, but then I consoled myself with the thought that, to enjoy it again, I would have to return to The Sign of the Angel, and that would be a special treat.

Lacock has proved to be an ideal setting for many film makers and we know that it has hosted a backdrop for films such as Moll Flanders, Pride and Prejudice, Cranford and Downton Abbey. However it has gained considerable fame as a setting for Harry Potter. I took the time to read The Chamber of Secrets and was impressed with the sophisticated level of the plot. Obviously youth engage well with this type of novel as, I may say, do many adults.

With more than 500 million copies of Harry Potter books sold, translations into 73 languages and a franchise estimated at $25 billion, the magical setting for Hogwarts School of Wizardry at Lacock Abbey, certainly establishes this venue as an international icon.

Life does not flit idly by at Lacock. On our last visit Ed and I were disappointed to find that the abbey and cloisters were closed as the area had been cordoned off for a new set of filming. Sadly, we missed rubbing shoulders with members of the cast as the filming contract was drawing to a close and everyone was moving off to the next venue. We asked staff at the National Trust what the new film was but everyone had been sworn to secrecy. However, a few days later I learned a little secret. Lacock had been the venue for some scenes of Fantastic Beasts number two!

Imagine having a beer in the local pub with Eddie Redmayne! He really is one of my favourite actors! I think I would also have enjoyed a chat with Johnny Depp. Well, whatever the unknown movie is, Lacock Abbey will once again provide an admirable scenic background for any mystery, drama, mythical tale or witchcraft scenario that needs the right atmosphere and character.

Lacock is one of the very special places to visit in Wiltshire. It is easily accessible and there is admirable provision for overnight stays, easy lunches or indulgent dining. Everyone enjoys those wonderful pathways into the past and I know they will invoke many happy memories in days that follow.

DEVIZES

Ed and I arrived in Devizes on one beautiful sunny September day and the remarkable weather belied the oncoming autumn season with its inevitable windy and overcast days. Our Sat-Nav guided us to the banks of the Kennet and Avon Canal, and while Ed made himself comfortable with a newspaper and a cup of coffee at the Black Horse *(left)* I set out to explore.

It was glorious walking along the canal waterway; there were no lurking clouds, not even a hint of a chilly breeze and I felt at peace with the world. School holidays were at an end and so the thoroughfare was relatively quiet

I viewed the stretch of waterway with interest and pondered how much a part of history it had once been. With an overall length of 87 miles this waterway connects the River Thames at Reading with the Avon River at Bath.

The main flight of 16 locks at Caen Hill on the Kennet and Avon Canal

With access to this canal, barges would once carry goods from Bristol to London. However the coming of the railways meant that the canal became redundant and it was only during the 1960s that a Trust was formed to save the channel and open it up for tourists and other travellers.

In 1990 the Kennet and Avon Canal was reopened and the Canal River Trust Organisation is now doing a splendid job in restoring the waterway.

I chatted to one of the Canal River Trust organisers and he spoke so enthusiastically about the work that was being done one can only surmise that extensive re-structuring will shortly result in wonderful achievements which will be of benefit not only to the town but the great number of tourists who make their way to Devizes.

A view of the lock gates

Page 53

I had a little chuckle as I wended my way along the canal path. A very visual notice gave strict instructions for no fishing in the vicinity; but there, tucked away neatly, and in a secluded and sheltered position, was a comfortable and unperturbed fisherman plying his trade on the river bank.

He was very well organised, with a little lunch box at his side, fishing tackle neatly arrayed and a smile of absolute pleasure as his line dangled idly in the water. He was probably enjoying the last of the summer sunshine with little or no concern about breaking the boundaries.

I shared his sunshine pleasure on return from my canal ramble and scrutinised the tour map as I made a decision on where I would go to for the next part of my exploration adventure.

Devizes has a fascinating history and in spite of early prehistoric settlements and evidence of Roman occupation it really came into its own with the building of a castle in Norman times. According to the Wiltshire Heritage Museum booklet, Devizes owes its name, existence and early history to this Norman Castle.

I was so excited to learn that there was a castle in the town. Imagine my disappointment to discover that it is now in private ownership and not accessible to the public. It was even more disappointing to find that the Castle was destroyed by Oliver Cromwell after the Battle of Roundway Down and the present one had been built in Victorian times. So much more history sadly lost!

The history of the castle is an intriguing one and I was fascinated with the struggle between Stephen and the Empress Matilda.

The present castle gateway

Who was Stephen and who was Matilda? They were cousins, both descended from William the Conqueror and both vied for control of the throne of England.

Devizes castle was a pivotal point in the struggle for the English crown between the two cousins.

Devizes Castle under siege

King Stephen

Empress Matilda

Matilda was the rightful heir to the English throne and Stephen had pledged to support her claim. However, when Henry I died, he reneged on his pledge, on the grounds that a woman should not take the throne.

He ruled England from 1135 until his death in 1154 but the period was one of civil strife and lawlessness. Possession of the castle was viewed as having command of the West Country and so numerous sieges ensued on the fortress.

After having to relinquish it to Stephen in 1139, Matilda won the town and the castle back in 1141. Henry II, Matilda's son, still had possession of the castle when he ascended the throne. This, with the surrounding parks, was later ceded to the crown.

The ill-fated castle was not to survive beyond another 500 years. At the outbreak of the civil war it was fortified to enable the Royalist forces to resist the Parliamentarians. The Battle of Roundway Down 1643 *(pictured right)* was a resounding victory for the Royalists under Lord Wilmot over the Parliamentarians under Sir William Waller. But with eventual supremacy of the Parliamentarians, Oliver Cromwell laid siege to the castle and demolished it.

Richard Holland in his book of Wiltshire ghost stories tells of a Cavalier who has been seen on the staircase striking a handsome pose on the staircase. Perhaps he is waiting to take his revenge on Cromwell.

Devizes prospered during the 18th century and from time to time enjoyed the fruits of illegal contraband. There is a delightful story of the Moonrakers whose story can be

seen in this Wiltshire postcard of 1903. Smuggling was particularly lucrative and some local citizens had hidden barrels of French brandy in a pond.

While trying to retrieve these one night they were apprehended by the revenue men. When asked for an explanation they showed the reflection of the moon on the pond and assured the excise men they were trying to rake in a round of cheese. Dismissed as foolish yokels they were left alone to continue salvaging their smuggled booty.

They must be admired for their quick thinking and ingenuity and Wiltshire men are called Moonrakers to this day.

Devizes grew in importance as a market town with essential trading products of wheat, wool and yarn. Today the town continues to flourish with its modern trade outlets but also benefits from a vibrant local market parading all manner of innovative merchandise.

The Corn Exchange on Market

Market Place

On a Saturday visit we were able to share in their happy market day. Shoppers surveyed the merchandise with interest and enthusiasm while vendors plied their trade in a professional and business-like manner. Meat, vegetables and breads were all on display as well as interesting stalls such as the Bee Centre, a weaving group, a basket stall, and even a small selection of livestock.

Everywhere happy crowds were observed chatting, sharing in some form of refreshment and generally enjoying the sunshine and festive atmosphere of the

trading centre. I am sure that this was how the market must have operated in the decades of the past.

What an excellent experience we enjoyed at Wadworth Brewery *(left)* as we wended our way, along with a tour group much younger than Ed and me. The tour leader was a chatty and knowledgeable lady who had first-hand experience with the brewing process.

She explained the ingredients which were barley, water, hops and yeast and let us taste some of the different barley grains. Then we toured the building to look at the various processes the mixture passes through before the final product is ready.

She took us into the sign writing room and explained that all the Wadworth signs were painted on site. Well over 300 of these signs are produced by the Wadsworth team and all are hand executed.

Hand-painted pub signs
Far left: The Penny Farthing
Near left: The Pelican

After the tour it was beer sampling time. We had half an hour for tasting the different brands. After savouring 1200 ml of diverse products I felt decidedly relaxed, a little light-headed and at peace with the world. At the end of the afternoon I had determined that my preferred choice of beverage was 6X and I bought myself a little 6X hat in the gift shop.

Wadworth uses horses to deliver their beer. What fun to see the famous Shire Horses out on the streets of Devizes on a weekday morning! I am sure there are many folk who greet them as they go on their daily rounds.

Our next exciting adventure was a visit to the wonderful Wiltshire Museum *(left)*. It is housed in Grade II Georgian and Victorian buildings and is open to visitors and researchers throughout the year.

The entrance is manned by a very serious Roman soldier whose presence demands respect and deference from all those who enter to view the incredible displays.

The Museum tells the story of prehistoric man, who lived in Wiltshire and could have built the World Heritage sites of Stonehenge and Avebury. It contains the largest selection of Early Bronze Age gold ever displayed in England. A finding of great significance quite close to Stonehenge is the

Bush Barrow site which is part of Normanton Downs Barrows cemetery. There was the discovery of a body with unusual artefacts, the most original being a large plate of gold in the form of a lozenge.

Apart from displays of Iron Age, Roman and Medieval history, the Museum also has a Saxon Gallery and a Story of Devizes Gallery. An Archive, Library and Art Gallery ensure that any persons wanting to do further research have the means to do so.

At the Museum:

A Roman legionary
A barrow entrance
Model of Bush Barrow
Model of Stonehenge

The Bear Inn *(left)* with its iconic black bear munching on a bunch of grapes, holds a prestigious position in the town centre.

I had determined that Ed and I would end a lovely Devizes day enjoying a tasty meal here. What more fitting than to join an elite host of guests, like King George III, Queen Charlotte and Edward VII who have been patrons through the ages. But sadly it was not meant to be. We were too late for lunch and evening meals were not available until 6 pm. I looked at their Christmas menus which seemed delicious and very reasonably priced.

During my canal walk I had been able to stop at the Caen Hill Café *(right)* and enjoy an ice-cream which went down very well while I sat out in a sun-drenched garden relishing my convivial surroundings.

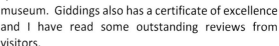

The café has been awarded a certificate of excellence. It is quaint, colourful and the staff members are friendly and accommodating; this is a really good place to visit.

Ed made use of Edwin Giddings *(left)* while I spent time in the museum. Giddings also has a certificate of excellence and I have read some outstanding reviews from visitors.

I haven't eaten there, but I am drawn to the Moonrakers *(below)* purely through the delightful legend. On my next visit to Devizes it will be my first port of call, especially as they appear to serve a well-presented, succulent steak.

I have no doubt that you will find much to do in Devizes and will thoroughly enjoy your visit.

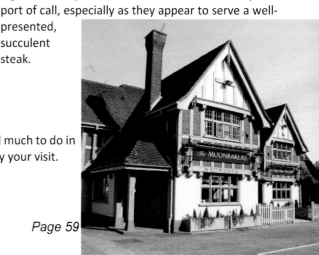

BRADFORD ON AVON

Having tea at the Bridge Tea Rooms in Bradford on Avon was one of the most important reasons for my visit to this very charming town in Wiltshire.

Accompanied by two dear friends, Gilly and Mal, and Ed my husband, we arrived at the Bridge Tea Rooms at noon. hoping to find a table before the lunch time rush ensued. We were escorted upstairs along a narrow-carpeted staircase to a comfortable little table for four.

There is a real sense of pageant in the quality of the rooms. Stone walls with areas of wooden panelling are features of the interior. A myriad of pictures framed with ornate gold and wooden borders adorn every area of wall space; the rooms simply radiate an era long past.

The building is a former blacksmith's cottage dating back to the 16th century. It changed hands over time until it finally gave way from an antique shop to these delightful Tea Rooms in the 20th century.

The table's lace cloth had an overlay of crisp white cotton and our young waitress was suitably attired in traditional Victorian apparel. Our tea was chosen from an amazing selection listed on their impressive, leather menus and was served in dainty, bone china crockery.

After enjoying a hearty breakfast, Ed and Mal were content with speciality tea and coffee, but Gilly and I tucked into a delicious Welsh Rarebit and salad meal. I had seen positive reviews about this menu choice and was determined to try it. Both Gilly and I gave it full marks for a light and appetising meal.

The Bridge Tea Rooms have achieved a fair measure of National acclaim and have on, several occasions, been awarded annual recognition as The Tea Guild's Top Tea Place. With all its charm and charisma and even a possible 'ghost' thrown in for good measure, it richly deserves this honour.

The 13th century bridge over the Avon which gives the town its name with the 17th century lock-up on the left-hand side.

If you gaze up the steep town hill, you will be aware of the many weavers' and spinners' cottages which rise level by level above the town. I have read that, if you have the energy to climb this hill, you will be rewarded with a breath-taking view of the whole area. I leave that pleasant undertaking to the energetic and the young at heart.

The small, chunky attachment on the ancient Norman Bridge was once a chapel, though I am not sure how many people could access this little place of worship. Perhaps it gained a more useful role as it became the lock-up venue for troublesome drunks who had imbibed too liberally.

My impression of this quaint town, which is focused around the famous bridge, was a haven of tranquillity and peacefulness.

The citizens of the town obviously pay great attention to the care of the community, as park areas and walkways are meticulously groomed.

The Avon meanders slowly on its journey to Bath. Pause for a moment and watch a swan dipping its head into the water to forage for a passing morsel, or found sending saucy ducks away in a scurry of flapping wings as they venture into forbidden territory.

Bradford on Avon developed as a centre of the woollen industry and many of the large buildings along the river were former woollen mills *(right, behind the bridge)*. These, I believe, are now converted to residential accommodation.

Shopping and unique restaurants are all there to tempt the tourist into interesting purchases and fine dining. Everywhere the feeling of history prevails and, although traffic poses a necessary encumbrance, the sense of serenity seems always present.

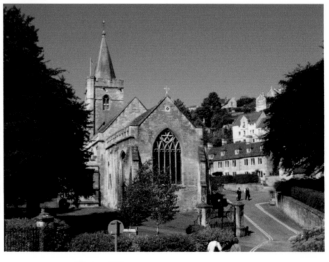

The Bridge Tea Rooms amongst other establishment on the corner of Bridge St and St Margaret's Street

Holy Trinity Church *(right)* dates from around the 12th century and, through the ages, has seen multiple changes. It stands amongst shady trees and its open doors invite all to enter and share its past and quiet reverence.

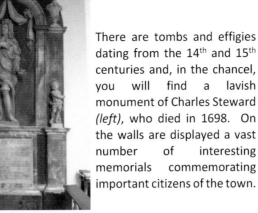

There are tombs and effigies dating from the 14th and 15th centuries and, in the chancel, you will find a lavish monument of Charles Steward *(left)*, who died in 1698. On the walls are displayed a vast number of interesting memorials commemorating important citizens of the town.

The inside of the huge tithe barn.
Photo courtesy of Michael Garlick

St Trinity's grounds

The grounds of the church, like the town itself, are carefully groomed, and the recent multimillion-pound refurbishment, has given Bradford a beautiful and well-loved church which is certainly worth a visit.

Photo courtesy of Charles Miller

The incredible Tithe Barn *(above left)* is of special interest, not only because it was used during the Middle Ages for the tithing of produce and livestock; it has also served as a film set for the television series of Robin Hood and for certain scenes in the film version of Canterbury Tales. It can be found at Barton Farm Country Park close to the town centre.

The famous 7th century St Laurence Church *(left)* is one of the few surviving Anglo-Saxon churches in England which has shown very little impact from rebuilding or renovations through the centuries. Under the auspices of the nuns of Shaftesbury Abbey it might have served as a mortuary chapel for King Edward the Martyr. The little church has been mentioned in the writings of William of Normandy.

The Kennett and Avon Canal *(right)* and the Bradford Lock have been wonderfully restored and are now in full working order. Visitors can organise river tours or simply stand by and watch the intricate manoeuvring of boats moving slowly through the locks or shifting round in the canal to return to base.

Besides its history and quaint charm, Bradford on Avon is an area of beautiful scenery and cycling and walking can be of immense pleasure to the visitor.

Great Chalfield Manor *(left and below)*, a National Trust property close to Bradford on Avon, is a most impressive 15th century house built for Thomas Tropenell. There are not many rooms to view and, the furnishings were, of necessity, restored in the 20th century, but the enduring sense of a long past heritage still lingers. If you shut your eyes and listen with care to the words of the excellent guide, you might well be immersed in the problems of civil war and how to circumvent the displeasure of either Lancastrian or Yorkist visitor.

As a matter of interest, the shrewd Thomas Tropenell had two sets of livery for his staff, one being Yorkist and the other Lancastrian, so when the alert was given there would be a rapid change of wearing apparel to suit respective visitors. We went through the Great Hall which certainly had a medieval flavour. I enjoyed seeing the 'spy holes' carefully positioned in the hall that allowed concerned members of the

household to view activities and personnel below and establish possible hidden agendas amongst guests.

Our guide told us of a bedtime legend. When the master and mistress were safely ensconced in their bed, two servants, one at either side, gripped the bed support ropes and pulled them tight before tucking in the occupants. Hence the expression, "Good night, sleep tight!" The priest had the dubious privilege of waking the family in the middle of the night for prayers – which required compulsory attendance of course.

What makes Great Chalfield Manor especially interesting was that it has been used for several BBC films, amongst them being Wives and Daughters 1999, the Other Boleyn Girl 2008, Tess of the d'Urbervilles 2008, Wolf Hall 2014 and last, but not least the Killewarran House in Poldark.

*The esplanaded (espalier) apple tree
at Great Chalfield Manor*

f you can include a visit to Great Chalfield Manor you will find it an inspiring and memorable inclusion to your Bradford on Avon destination.

THE HISTORIC MARKET TOWN OF CHIPPENHAM

Through the ages Chippenham has always been noted as an important market town and, besides its access to the River Avon, it was strategically based on the Bristol to London road.

The little medieval town was probably founded in AD 600 by Anglo-Saxons although there are obvious signs of Roman occupation before then.

In the 9th century Chippenham was under the rule of Alfred who had to contend with Danish raiders whom he eventually defeated. He had allowed them to settle in Eastern and Northern sections of England which became known as Danelaw.

Ed and I decided to explore this historic town for ourselves and set out on Bus 55 which travels from Swindon to Chippenham

Chippenham Town Hall

Our route took us via Royal Wootton Bassett, Lyneham and Calne and we rode through stunning, lush, green countryside. The bus ride was pleasant and we enjoyed seeing another part of wonderful Wiltshire. It was a beautiful summer's day in August and Chippenham was in full bloom. We joined the crowds of shoppers who hurried through the market area tempted by a vast display of enticing food and alluring apparel.

This little metal calf *(left)* is positioned strategically in the walk-way of Borough Parade. His presence shows the importance Chippenham once had as one of the largest cattle markets in the country. Cattle are no longer visible in the market area, but other four-legged friends certainly are, and two horses with their amicable riders *(right)* spent time with curious shoppers and entertained the children who delighted in their tame friendship.

Market stalls *(above)*, which function on Fridays and Saturdays, certainly have a firm following with the locals. The banter, the chatter and the laughter, evident throughout the area, are indicative of a thriving financial trading system which must have an important impact on the community.

Imagine what this town once looked like – simple, orderly, functional! Has it changed very much over the decades or even centuries? I don't think so. Perhaps the trappings of modern civilization and culture have bedecked the markets with gaudy promotional materials, but the substance of the town still breathes through its solid foundations.

Chippenham High Street and Avon Bridge
(Thanks to Chippenham Museum for permission to use the photographs)

The passer-by can gaze with the mind's eye and visualise a past that rolls back through the centuries to a little settlement on the banks of the Avon, in existence well before Roman times.

The Buttercross on the right has a strange history. Used in the 16th century for the sale of meat and dairy products, it was dismantled and taken to Castle Coombe, and then returned to its place of honour at the top of the market in 1995.

The Grade 1 listed Yelde Hall *(right)*, is a timber framed Medieval Town Hall. The space below the Council Chamber was used as the town gaol.

The wonderful old Bear Inn *(below)* is magnificent in its prime position in the heart of the town. Perhaps a little run down but still very stately, and it even boasts a few ghosts who enjoy presiding noisily inside unoccupied rooms and then simply disappearing whenever members of staff arrive to investigate their unruly behaviour.

I paid a visit to the magnificent St Andrew's Church and admired its modern seating arrangements.

A lady was busy preparing rows of coffee cups and I asked her if she was expecting visitors that afternoon – but she informed me that this was preparation for the Sunday services. Good organisation, St Andrew's Ladies! She told me about their plans for a new servery and I replied that there were similar expectations at St Mary's, Purton. The church is used as a facility for concerts and other functions which means that it is very much at the heart of community activity. I noticed a cosy corner for the small fry – a safe place to keep them occupied during liturgical formalities.

St Andrew's is probably on the site of a Saxon Church which was rebuilt in the 15th century with further renovations in the 18th century when the roof was raised and the chancel extended. It is very likely that King Alfred's sister and possibly even his

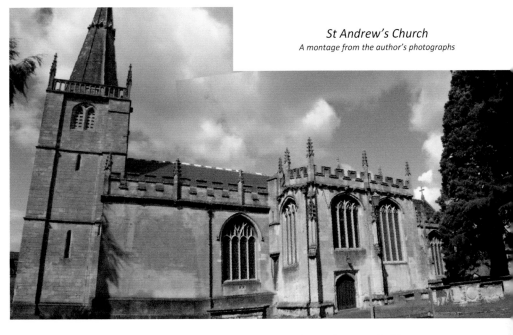

St Andrew's Church
A montage from the author's photographs

St Andrew's crèche area (left)
and the chancel (below)

daughter were wedded here. I was moved to read about the tragic loss of three sons of the Wilson family in WW1. They have commemorated this deep sadness with a beautiful stained glass window in the church.

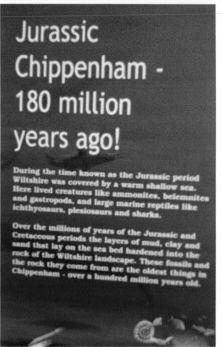

Jurassic Chippenham - 180 million years ago!

During the time known as the Jurassic period Wiltshire was covered by a warm shallow sea. Here lived creatures like ammonites, belemnites and gastropods, and large marine reptiles like ichthyosaurs, plesiosaurs and sharks.

Over the millions of years of the Jurassic and Cretaceous periods the layers of mud, clay and sand that lay on the sea bed hardened into the rock of the Wiltshire landscape. These fossils and the rock they come from are the oldest things in Chippenham - over a hundred million years old.

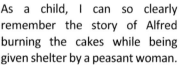

Photo – Betty Longbottom

The Chippenham Museum *(above)* is a wealth of information and tells the story of the town from the very earliest of times right up until the 21st century. Imagine Chippenham being covered by a warm shallow sea millions of years ago and all that mud, clay and sand hardening into the rock of the Wiltshire landscape.

Alfred stands quietly in the little museum gazing thoughtfully into the portals of time *(right)*. But he wasn't always quiet and on a previous visit he actually spoke to me, which I found rather disconcerting until I realized that his voice was a recording. King Alfred was born at Wantage in Oxfordshire but probably had a hunting lodge in Chippenham. King's Lodge School in Chippenham is so named as it is thought that the hunting lodge stood near the site of the school

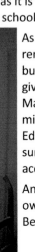

As a child, I can so clearly remember the story of Alfred burning the cakes while being given shelter by a peasant woman. Maybe it was her scolding which prompted him into further military action and led to the defeat of a Danish army at Edington. The survivors fled to Chippenham and surrendered, with the leader of the Danes, Guthrum, accepting Christianity and being baptised.

Another gentleman with whom I am familiar was our very own Isambard Kingdom Brunel *(in the display left)*. Because I live very close to Swindon, I have been on countless trips to the Steam Museum and also visited the Museum Ship of the SS Great Britain in Bristol. She was designed by Brunel and when launched in 1843 was the largest vessel afloat. I frequently chat to Brunel about his wonderful achievements. He tends to stay very quiet and let me do all the talking.

Although Chippenham was part of the Wilts & Berks Canal, it was the Great Western Railway which finally had a dynamic effect on the town. Brunel's viaduct *(right)* was to carry the G W Railway over the town and trains would run through Chippenham from London to Bristol. The arrival of the railway in 1841 prompted an extensive growth of industries which also necessitated an expansion of housing. It also heralded a new way of life. The droving of sheep and cattle, under the viaduct in the engraving, didn't last much longer.

There is a large military display in the museum explaining how the people of Chippenham were involved in the war effort and how they contributed to the defence of their country. A visit to the museum will be an informative and enriching experience.

The River Avon is a popular venue for riverside walks and fishing and visitors are attracted to enjoy its gentle flow.

The River Avon at Chippenham flowing in from Malmesbury on its way towards Bath and the sea at Avonmonth.

We chose to have a late lunch at the Rivo Lounge on the River Avon. It is an interesting restaurant decorated in an Art Deco style with lots of mirrors and old pictures.

Ed and I enjoyed the atmosphere. I was hungry and chose a burger with all the trimmings while Ed had Eggs Benedict *(below also with the interior)*. He was so impressed with his meal that he informed the Management he would be back for more. We were fortunate that a No 55 Bus stop was right outside the restaurant so we could rest full tummies by sitting quietly and bathing in the sun before our transport arrived.

There is much to interest the visitor to Chippenham. Delightful gift shops, restaurants, pubs and coffee shops abound and everything is so easily accessible. Not too far away

are the historic sites of Castle Coombe and Lacock.

There are excellent visiting opportunities in and around Chippenham. Sheldon Manor is an interesting historic house. This is Wiltshire's oldest inhabited manor dating back to Saxon times. House and Gardens are occasionally open to the public.

Sheldon Manor
Photo by Roger-Cornfoot

Corsham Court *(above)* is a beautiful stately home and is open to the public with guided tours.

The parklands surrounding the gardens of Bowood House *(below)* were designed by 'Capability' Brown in the 1760s, so there will be much to enjoy for those who love the rich flora and fauna of a beautifully landscaped estate.

Bowood House is also acclaimed for its children's adventure playground, its renowned golf course and its exclusive hotel.

Chippenham is part of Wonderful Wiltshire and you certainly must certainly plan a visit here.

A VISIT TO AVEBURY

I have visited Avebury on three occasions, with friends and family, and each time I have come away stunned at the enormity of this vast primordial backdrop which dates back into the mists of time.

Who were these ancient inhabitants who graced the plains of once unblemished Wiltshire Downs? Were they Aliens who found their way from Mars, a planet showing similar physical signs of the Henge structures, or were they an early group of primal dwellers, ordered and structured, simple in life style but already conscious of community interdependence?

History assures us that these early people were our ancestors, but it is interesting to wonder if indeed they were.

Possible construction method
Picture from Avebury Museum

However, we can certainly gaze in awe and wonder at engineering skill and expertise which allowed these pioneers of antiquity to achieve the inconceivable.

One of the massive stones

An aerial view of Avebury is available through Photo Websites, and shows the vicinity with clarity. By viewing from above it is evident how unobtrusively the little village mushroomed right into the centre of these giant monuments and became the only village to be contained within a sarsen (hard form of sandstone) structure.

An aerial view of the village and its stones
English Heritage Trust picture

Avebury is one of the best-known prehistoric areas in Britain. Together with Stonehenge it is a world heritage site with the largest megalithic stone circle in the world and attracts visitors who range from enthusiastic tourists and archaeologists to contemporary pagans. One of the ways that Avebury differs from Stonehenge is that the visitor is free to touch the stones. The warmth of a tangible energy is experienced by many who seem to share the feelings of mystical allegiance to the thousands who trod these ancient paths.

Windmill Hill was the earliest known settlement in the area, probably built around 3700 BC and remaining in use until about 2500 BC.

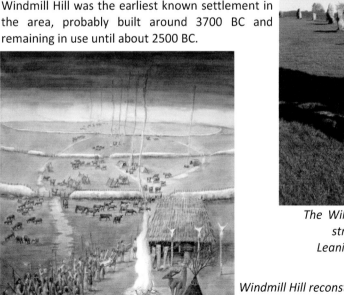

The Wiltshire equivalent of straightening the Leaning Tower of Pisa?

Windmill Hill reconstruction by Judith Dobie
Avebury Monuments Teacher's Kit

75

On one of my visits, I was accompanied by Ed and my two sisters Sandy and Chloe. We made the trip to West Kennet long barrow, but only two staunch explorers, Sandy and I, finally got to the top of the hill. Whenever a monument, such as this ancient barrow is approached, it is always with a sense of wonder, and one cannot help but project back in time to connect with the silent mourners as they move through their ancient burial rituals.

West Kennet, the longest chambered tomb in the country *(above)*, has its origins in around about 3000 BC.

Sandy *(left)* felt drawn to its cool dark chamber and she sensitively shared the strange, historic reverence engendered by the tomb.

Another unexplained phenomenon is the ancient structure of Silbury Hill *(below)*. Featuring as the largest prehistoric man-made hill in Europe and dating back to about 2450 BC, it can be compared in height and volume to the Egyptian pyramids.

But what was its purpose and significance? Why did those ancient occupants spend between 140 to 435 years structuring this hill? For a development venture such as this, continued over centuries, there must have been strong motivation and it is probably grounded in ancestral veneration.

Silbury Hill is not a burial ground; archaeological diggings and research have proved this. What then? Alone it stands in splendid isolation, still a stark reminder of a mysterious past. In its origins, the chalk dug from ditches to expand and enlarge its formation, would have exposed a barren, white image.

However, over time traditional ceremonies obviously waned and the area become overgrown and neglected.

The Avebury stone circle itself probably dates from about 2500 BC, so is not as old as Windmill Hill. Its great outer circle once held about 100 enormous standing stones.

Inside this large area stood two smaller circles! Perhaps more impressive than the great circles of stone are the banks of the Henge earthworks surrounding them! How incredible to think that the ditches about 9 metres deep and 10 metres wide could be cut into the underlying chalk by people having no excavation equipment.

It is thought that about 200,000 tons of chalk rubble were hauled up to create the banks of the Henge.

Sadly, this wonderful area appears to have been abandoned in the Iron Age and apart from evidence of a Roman presence, activity is not seen again until the early middle ages when a village began to materialise.

In the late Middle Ages and early Modern periods, sections of the Avebury monument were destroyed. Without realising their precious heritage, village folk were using the stones to build cottages and storage areas.

In the winter of 1649 John Aubrey, a young Wiltshire gentleman, was hunting with friends, when he discovered the Avebury Henge. He was intrigued and began work on gathering information for a natural historical and antiquarian pre-history study. His sustained efforts aroused a great deal of interest and contributed to bringing the prehistoric site of Avebury to public attention.

John Aubrey
picture from Wikipedia

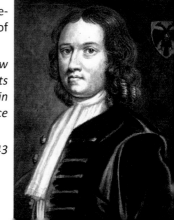

William Stukeley *(below right, a self portrait of 1735)* started his career in medicine and then became a clergyman, but it is his invaluable record of the Avebury monument to which we are indebted and his detailed observations helped to provide evidence of a valuable pre-historic site for the benefit of those who were to follow his investigations.

He wrote: *Therefore I thought it fully worthwhile, to bestow some pains on these temples of theirs as the only monuments we have left, of the patriarchal religion; and especially in regard to their extraordinary grandeur and magnificence equal to any of the wonders of the world.*

William Stukeley, 'Abury' 1743

Wonderful Wiltshire

Alexander Keiller is largely responsible for much of the restoration of Avebury today. Known as the Marmalade Man, from a family business started in the late 18th century, he acquired enormous wealth which enabled him to pursue a rich and varied life and enjoy immeasurable success.

Alexander Keiller
photo National Trust

His keen interest in archaeology prompted him to buy Windmill Hill, 2 miles from Avebury, and between 1925 and 1929 he set out to undertake a series of excavations unearthing a causewayed enclosure.

Most sarsens in Avebury had long since toppled over or were buried by farmers or Christians, fearful of the supernatural.

After a careful investigation of the Henge he excavated and re-erected the stones which had lain buried in the earth into their original holes, mainly on the western side of the circle, and, where stones were missing, he marked the spot with concrete pillars. Many cottages and farms within the Great Henge were knocked down to accommodate his stone circle.

World War II brought further work to an end and failing health prevented any additional activity in his endless archaeological pursuits.

Keiller was an extraordinary gentleman. Filled with incredible verve and energy he embarked on a varied and intensive lifestyle from helping to pioneer aerial photography, searching for the Loch Ness monster, becoming President of the Ski Club of Great Britain, becoming a skilled marksman, studying criminology which enabled him, during WW2, to become expert in fingerprints, founding the Sizaire-Berwick auto company and assembling his own fleet of sleek, shiny cars.

His good looks and congenial nature made him popular, especially with the ladies.

However, he will always be remembered for his passion for archaeology and his restoration of a World Heritage site.

The Manor House *(left)* is a Grade 1 Listed building dating back to the 16th century. It had several owners, and it was probably William Duntch, a wealthy courtier and Auditor for the Royal Mint who rebuilt the house to the structure which we can see today.

Final changes came to the house in the early 20th century when a library and beautiful gardens were added by the Jenner family.

Although hard times forced them to sell their house, Avebury was so beloved by them that they chose to be buried in a small area of the manor gardens, now consecrated as part of the churchyard. Alexander Keiller bought the house in 1937 and used it while embarking on his archaeological exploits. He sold the house in 1955 and it eventually became part of the National Trust in 1991.

The BBC used the house for a television series 'The Manor Reborn' and they completely restored and refurbished it *(right)*. This helped to showcase the manor house and boosted its popular appeal.

The Anglo-Saxon church of St James *(pictured left)* still retains its original nave, although slightly altered by the Normans. Various changes throughout the centuries structured the building as a comfortable place of worship for the village folk. It is securely nestled in its little churchyard and, although not boasting the antiquity of its monolithic surrounds, still adds a significant aura of the past.

The High Street consists of quaint thatched cottages *(right)*, with the usual tourist shops where a host of memorabilia items can be purchased.

The National Trust has its own tourist shop and restaurant together with the famous Alexander Keiller

museum in the Barn Gallery *(left)*. It details his archaeological work and has one of the best displays of prehistoric remains in the country.

As a licensed pub since 1802, the Red Lion *(right)* has become a firm favourite with locals and visitors.

It has gained fame for being the only pub in the world set in the centre of a prehistoric stone monument; it has also gained the dubious honour of being the most haunted pub in the world.

Strange activities occur, like a swinging chandelier when any bearded gent passes in the vicinity, or missing bar items which disappear and, without explanation, mysteriously appear again, and the presence of two terrified children cringing in the corner of a hotel room while an indifferent lady ignores their presence, or a cold spirit that moves through a sleeper's domain on the very hottest of nights.

There are visitors who are sensitive to the supernatural and have been known to leave the inn refusing to ever return. Pub owners disassociate themselves from the phantom carriage drawn by ghostly horses that clatter through the courtyard, as their spectral presence is usually an omen of tragedy.

Of course, the most famous ghost of all is the wicked Florrie whose body was stuffed into the well by her husband. This well is now a very smart bar table with a glass top *(left)*, and the customers using it at the time of my visit were very happy for me to take this photo. The story of the naughty lady relates to any cuckolded husband who returns form military duty to find his wife in the arms of a lover. In vengeful style the lover was shot and Florrie duly had her throat cut. But Florrie is still about, so you should be watchful.

Avebury is such a mingled merge of the mystical and material that you will find yourself walking through an exciting encounter with the past. Your visit will furnish you with wonderful memories and you will want to return, either to relive that pleasure, or to search for greater depth of understanding.

MARLBOROUGH
A Historic Town of Character and Charm

This aerial view of the town by Brian Robert Marshall was taken at the top of St Peter's Church Tower.
(The photo is licensed for reuse under Creative Commons Licence).

This is a wonderful panorama of the town with its extensive High Street. It is here that activity is at its most intense and embodies the pulse and throb of the town. If you look beyond the built-up area you will see that Marlborough stretches into a lush green landscape. When Ed and I made our way home via the Broad Hinton road we sat in absolute silence and were completely mesmerised by the beautiful countryside.

What makes Marlborough special and why do visitors return again and again? I think perhaps it is the charm of its unique trading area. The shops, boutiques, restaurants and pubs along the High Street are a welcoming and friendly collection of vendors offering merchandise and services of quality and gratification. Let us look more closely at how the High Street unravels and invites the visitor to enjoy its wares and participate in its diversions.

Standing in superior isolation at the top of the High Street is this beautiful town hall *(right)* which is rather young in comparison with many of the other buildings. Structured in the favourite Dutch style of the Edwardians, it was only completed in 1902. However it is a very imposing building and stands like a sentinel on an insular summit looking broodily over the rest of its domain.

The Bear at Marlborough *(right)* is a stunning 18th century inn which has served for centuries as a respite for weary folk travelling between London and South Wales.

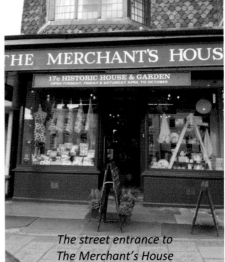

There was always a warm fire, a good meal and a tankard of ale to settle the traveller down for the night.

Tucked around the back of the town hall is a narrow street *(left)* with quaint little shops rising uphill into a flight of entrepreneurial delights. The shopping in Marlborough just goes on and on.

One of my great pleasures in exploring Marlborough was to share in the mysteries of the Merchant House. I joined a 12 pm. tour one Tuesday and was, in fact, the only member of the party, so I had the tour guide all to myself.

What a warm, friendly and interesting person she was. The guide was absolutely passionate about the house and, as she expounded in detail on the secrets being uncovered in the renovation process, I felt an intense response to every aspect of the story.

After the Great Fire of Marlborough, this 17th century house was rebuilt by Thomas Bayly, a prosperous silk merchant, and was to remain a family dwelling until 1731.

At this time it submitted to tenancy occupation and then over the years began a long association with printing tradesmen.

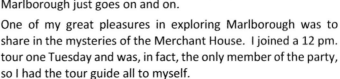

In 1991 it was set up as The Merchant's House Trust and with careful restoration is becoming a wonderful town attraction for visitors.

We started off our tour in the kitchen and examined a number of interesting cooking utensils. I loved this cheese grater *(bottom left)*; I imagine the cheese would flake off into long skinny tendrils.

The street entrance to The Merchant's House

The main stair well has slowly been restored and is assuming a little of its previous glory.

Thomas Bayly was a widely travelled man and must have enjoyed collecting artefacts as he journeyed into distant countries. My guide coveted the

beautiful chair *(right)* in his study – not the original from this household – but certainly of the same time period. She also loved his little cabinet which housed a wide ranging collection of spices. As she opened each draw the spicy odours wafted tantalisingly through the room evoking pleasant reminders of Christmas festivities.

Records have revealed that Thomas Bayly's dining room was richly embellished with 12 Turkeywork chairs. At one time these were very fashionable in England but they quickly fell from grace and their disappearance has now made them extremely rare furnishings. It is to the credit of the Trust that they were able to replicate these through the efforts of superior craftsmen.

Please note the wall decor of vertical stripes on a green background. Look closely at the floorboards – they are made from wide elm planks and it is incredible that they have stood the test of time so well.

I was greatly entertained by the privy which is secreted adjacent to the panelled chamber. It had a wooden seat and a drop-in pewter liner with definite ventilation visible at the top of the door. I don't think perfumed toilet sprays were available in those days – but you never know.

I enjoyed my visit enormously and I am sure that others will have as much pleasure in walking for an hour and a half through the pages of history.

The well-restored dining room in The Merchant's House

Wonderful Wiltshire

Continuing along the High Street there are an intriguing number of interesting retail outlets. I was surprised by the many hair salons – residents obviously take a keen interest in their appearance and aim to look as well-groomed as possible.

I peeped into the Polly Tea Rooms *(right)*. How

delightful! Patrons were enjoying superior service in a vintage type atmosphere which boasted delectable classic dishes served by elegant waitresses.

I learned from the Polly Tea Rooms Website that this was a favourite haunt of Kate Middleton when she attended Marlborough College as a student. I also learned that the establishment was started by two ladies, Miss Jean Leith Hay and Miss Janet McCloud (an original suffragette) in 1912 and many of their recipes are still in use today.

Of course, Ed and I had to sample their breakfast menu which we did a few days later. We enjoyed the atmosphere, the feeling of stepping into the past, the delicious Eggs Benedict and the beautifully served breakfast tea.

Couldn't stay for afternoon tea, but it looked tempting.

According to the Gazette and Herald of 5 November 2017, Marlborough ranks among the top ten attractions in almost 1000 shopping areas. This can only be because the retailers provide quality and 'award winning' shops to serve a discerning community

To add to the profusion of intriguing merchandise available on the High Street, there is also access to colourful market stalls every Wednesday and Saturday. Their interesting and delectable wares provide fascinating scope for tempting retail purchases and their existence is an integral part of community life with trading outlets occupying a vast area right in the middle of the town.

At the far end of the High Street is the imposing St Peter's Church *(left)*, no longer used for religious worship, but still a vigorous and energetic community establishment where patrons can enjoy a home cooked meal of fish and chips or beef pie, or perhaps a bowl of hot soup. There is a breakfast menu and a delicious afternoon tea menu.

St Mary's is the second church in Marlborough and stands behind the town hall. By 1970 it became obvious that the parish was unable to support two congregations and, as St Mary's was larger and in a better state of repair, it was decided to make St Peter's redundant and find an alternative use for the church and so preserve this wonderful historic building.

The Mayor, Alderman Jake Seamer led the way in establishing a Trust to care for St Peters and there it stands rich in community life and wonderfully preserved history.

Above: St Peter's Church.

Right: the teashop inside the nave.

Below: one of its many craft stalls.

Merlin is the legendary wizard who is best known in Arthurian legend and medieval Welsh poetry. There are many accounts of his death and burial with some writers believing he was bewitched and taken from Arthur by the Lady of the Lake, as seen in this picture, The Beguiling of Merlin by Edward Burne-Jones *(left)*.

The people of Marlborough have different ideas. They believe that the remains of Merlin lie right here in their own little civic borough. How exciting to think that somewhere in the mists of time the legendary wizard Merlin was buried in the precincts of what is now Marlborough College.

The Merlin Mound is carefully preserved in the College grounds and carbon dating takes it back to 2400 BC. English Heritage have found the new discovery as '... a very exciting time for British prehistory.'

Marlborough Mound was used as a castle from Norman times until it lay in ruins and in 1403 was replaced by a stately home. Eventually it became a coaching Inn and finally culminated in the prestigious Marlborough College which was established in 1843.

Savernake Forest *(below)* is about a mile from Marlborough and is a privately-owned estate, although large sections are open to the public. It has been designated an area of outstanding natural beauty and is well worth a visit.

Wikipedia tells us that Henry VIII visited Savernake and there became enamoured of

his host's daughter, Jane Seymour. With the inevitable execution of Anne Boleyn, Henry and Jane were soon married. Sadly she died giving birth to Edward VI. Sir John Seymour, and later his two sons, now became leading role players in the Tudor dynasty.

The Marlborough Downs, which are a part of the North Wessex Downs, have also been designated an area of outstanding natural beauty, and if you can plan a drive in the area, I am sure you will find it a pleasurable adventure.

Avebury is about 10 minutes away from Marlborough by car, 30 minutes by bus, and is a National Trust location that will give enormous pleasure to the visitor. There is an opinion that the Merlin Mound is the little sister to Silbury Hill in Avebury. An interesting supposition and, as time unravels,, the truth may yet be learned.

Ed and I explored Avebury in the previous chapter which describes our delightful encounters in that prehistoric village.

Wiltshire has so many wonderful towns and villages to enjoy, and a start in Marlborough will give you a taste of extraordinary things to come.

SALISBURY

No matter how familiar we might be with the history, life and legends of Salisbury, our minds revert immediately to one important manifestation of this vibrant city and that is the splendid Cathedral which majestically dominates the surrounding parkland and business centre. I have visited Salisbury on several occasions and each time my mind is overawed by this spectacular edifice.

The origins of the city lie on its outskirts and they reach back well into prehistory where later an iron-age fort in the area was taken over by the Saxons after their defeat of the Celts. However it was William the Conqueror who really brought Old Sarum into the limelight. He strengthened its defences and built himself an imposing castle where he and his successors, from time to time, took up residence.

Ed and I visited Old Sarum on a hot July morning. Rain clouds were building up and I was sure a welcome shower was on the way. Although extremely hot, it was quiet and peaceful with only a couple of family groups enjoying picnics next to the old castle and revelling in the scenic beauty from the hilltop.

A walk around the ruins *(pictures above)* will transport you into a medieval time zone. Amble slowly around and visualise a foundling abbey overshadowed by a mighty military force. Imagine the stress of running your abbey under the fierce control of the man who conquered Britain.

So, who would dominate the hilltop settlement, church or military? If Harold and the English army couldn't survive against William the Conqueror, what chance did Bishop Richard Poore have?

David Hilliam in his book, *Salisbury A Miscellany*, gives several reasons why the clergy sought to establish a new Cathedral site. Old Sarum had no room for expansion. The hilltop was windy and there was a desperate scarcity of water. The clergy were humiliated when they absented themselves from the fort at Rogationtide (an old

A model showing how Old Sarum might have looked in the 13th century

church festival) and returned to find they were locked out of Old Sarum. With nowhere to go except the banks of the hilltop, they waited in seething indignation throughout the night, enduring the laughter and jeers from soldiers on the castle walls.

Although the Cathedral in the Norman Garrison had been built in 1075 by Bishop St Osmund, it was not until 1217 that a final move was negotiated between Bishop

Richard Poore *(left)* and the Pope. The clergy would abandon the fort for a more suitable location two miles away on the banks of the Avon.

I was intrigued with Bishop Poore who appeared to be a man of determination and vision. He created a new town to house the workers for his Cathedral so that streets were laid out in a grid pattern which differs from the random thoroughfares of medieval towns.

The fact that the Cathedral was built with a purpose, achieving completion in 38 years, meant that it followed a set design and achieved a unity of structure never previously conceived.

The Cathedral is built on marshland with a high water table. Our tour guide dropped a measuring stick through a hole in the Cathedral floor to explain that water was not far distant from the foundations. He swivelled the stick inside the aperture so we could hear the lapping liquid. In an exceptionally heavy rainy season, water rises up on to the floor of the nave. Subsistence of the building is a constant danger and is always being monitored.

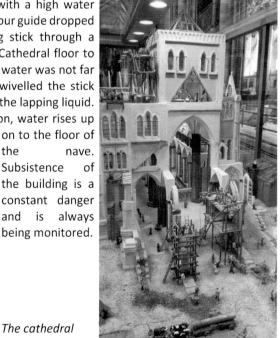

The cathedral West Front and spire

A model showing the construction techniques of the new cathedral.

Wonderful Wiltshire

Before starting on my tour, Ed and I treated ourselves to a cup of coffee in the Restaurant, and here we met up with Revd. Margaret Jones *(on the right in the picture)*. She gave me a great deal of information about historic sites to visit in Salisbury. She also told me that

I would enjoy a visual marvel when I entered the Cathedral.

She was right! What a stunning experience to view hundreds of doves in flight! I needed to sit down for a few moments to follow their silent and graceful route to the high altar. This exhibition was initiated to mark the centenary of the end of World War One. Similar exhibitions have featured in other major cities.

The artist, Michael Pendry has encouraged community groups to fold their own doves. He says: *"Although the doves are folded by different people, in their unity they stand for a fundamental human right - the right to peace and freedom. The time has come to declare ourselves and to stand up for this! May the flock of doves grow, from place to place, from country to country, and across all borders. Peace, freedom, and sustainability in a world of change and disturbance are the key themes of my installations."*

Our tour of the Cathedral started with a look at the Wiltshire Regimental Colours *(right)* which hang on the North Wall. Colours are no longer carried in battle but they remain a compelling reminder and symbol of the Regiment's devotion to duty. The Colours may never be mended but hang in their original condition as retrieved from the battlefield.

Plaques on the wall commemorate the Regiment's participation in the Anglo Boer War.

The mechanical monstrosity, on the right, chugs cheerfully away at its laboured process of time keeping. The guide proudly informed us that this is the oldest clock in the world. I listened carefully for ticking and tried to count the time rotation of the wheels, and it certainly didn't correspond to seconds so I can't truthfully tell you how it works.

Its claim to fame was that it was built in 1386 and its purpose was to ring a bell on the hour to remind parishioners of service times. This important ritual act reminds me nostalgically of my convent boarding school days when we were summoned by repetitive chimes to Evensong or Holy Mass.

Building started on the Cathedral in 1220 but the design was conceived without a spire. When this was added to the Cathedral between 1334 and 1363, at 404 feet it dominated the area and was visible for miles around; but the tower came at a cost.

The foundations were not designed to carry the extra weight of over 6000 tons.

Planning a system of support must be attributed to the ingenuity of craftsmen, architects and builders who, without access to modern technology had to rely on intelligence, acumen and experience.

Wonderful Wiltshire

Our tour leader made each of us look up into the buttress supports.

'Do stone pillars bend?' he asked. Well, for all to clearly see *(right)*, the stone pillars were bending. The only reason why the tower is still standing is because additional buttresses and masonry girders now give it the necessary support.

How beautiful is this Cathedral! There is serenity and peacefulness within its majestic arches and visitors move in restrained appraisal of all the beauty on offer.

Ed and I sat in to enjoy part of Evensong. As most of the service is vocal we felt enriched by the splendid choral presentation. Voices rose in stirring unison and echoed through the heights of the lofty tower in a strangely haunting refrain.

Majestic arches (left & centre) and the chorister stalls in the Choir

There are a great many tombs within the Cathedral but my favourite and most visited is that of William Longespee *(left)*. Why? Well he married and was deeply attached to the lovely Countess Ela of Lacock Abbey fame – he was a good husband a fine soldier and an important part of Cathedral beginnings. William never fully recovered from a near shipwreck disaster and on his return to England he died shortly after. His was the first tomb in the cathedral.

There are some historians who believe he had been poisoned and when his tomb was opened in 1791 the corpse of a perfectly preserved rat was found in his skull. Examinations revealed traces of arsenic in the rat. It makes you think doesn't it?

By far the most magnificent tomb in the cathedral *(left)* is that of Sir Edward Seymour and Lady Katherine Grey, sister to Lady Jane Grey. Theirs was a secret wedding and when it was discovered that they had married without royal consent, Elizabeth I committed them both to The Tower.

In spite of their prison separation two sons were born to her during their captivity. Sadly Katherine would never leave The Tower. In deep depression she pined away and died 8 years after their marriage. Seymour was finally released and, although he married again, it was his express wish to be buried alongside Katherine. So there they lie peacefully together with her in a raised position to denote her link to Royalty.

If you walk along the magnificent Cloister *(left)* to the Chapter House you will encounter one of the most significant treasures of the Cathedral. Here, in a protective awning, is one of four original copies of the Magna Carta *(right)*.

Of course, each one in our group was eager to view this ancient document so we stepped in tentatively to gaze in wonder. It is small, mellowed with age and covered with the minutest print I have ever seen. The scribe was probably a monk from the church and he must have been skilled in the craft of calligraphic script.

Wonderful Wiltshire

Eight hundred years old the Magna Carta still has a major influence in our lives today. It has established the principle that everyone is subject to the law and guarantees the rights of the individual.

It has influenced the American Bill of Rights and the Universal Declaration of Human Rights put in place after WW2.

Leaving the hustle and bustle of the city you can access the beautiful and serene Cathedral Close through the Grade 1 listed building of North Gate *(right)*. It is such a unique entrance that passing through its portals inspires a distinct sensation of stepping back into time and if you loiter awhile you will see visitor after visitor eagerly flashing away with cameras to capture its atmospheric quality.

Once inside the Close it is time to enjoy, not only the splendid manicured lawns and lofty trees but also a host of magnificent historic houses and attractions.

I visited Mompesson House *(left)* which is an elegant Queen Anne mansion built in 1701 for Sir Thomas Mompesson, an MP for Salisbury.

It is a well-appointed and gracious establishment with fine plaster work on the ceilings and stairways and superior antique furniture. It even had its own flight of doves ascending the stairs *(below right)*.

Mompesson House is a Grade 1 listed building and after being in the possession of a number of owners during the next 250 years was eventually given to the National Trust who has opened up the gracious residence to the public.

Above centre: Mompesson House viewed from The Close.

Right: furnishings in one of the bedrooms.

Far right: the staircase with folded doves.

Arundells *(right)* is another superb house to visit and I spent a pleasurable afternoon going through a residence which looked as if it was freshly opened and waiting for the return of the absentee family.

Although the first recorded occupant was the Archdeacon of Dorset in 1291 it finally became the home of Edward Heath who lived there for the last 20 years of his life. It is a warm and friendly home with evidence of memorabilia in all the rooms.

I was allowed to sample fine hors- d'oeuvres at his table.

Right is Edward's favourite chair and it afforded a most welcome rest in my busy pursuit of the house. His cartoon display is entertaining and the many gifts from people such as Sir

Winston Churchill are an indication of his fascinating public life. He obviously enjoyed music and photos and trophies of his yachting successes are widely visible.

The Close is a treasure trove of magnificent buildings and one that must be visited is the Grade 1 listed museum *(right)* which is renowned for its archaeological collection. Members of staff there are helpful and informative and go out of their way to chat about the exhibits. I visited the museum in 2017 and was intrigued by the display of Stonehenge Art. I took out my camera to photograph

some innovative work when a gentle tap on my shoulder halted my efforts. No photographs of the exhibits please! I should have known that.

The Poultry Cross *(left)* is a picturesque edifice which marks the spot of almost 700 years of market trading in Salisbury.

Markets ancient and modern

Market days are every Tuesday and Saturday and there is vibrancy and a noisy vitality throughout the market area. I thoroughly enjoyed the business and energy, as stall holders call out to shoppers encouraging them to sample their wares. I even found a South African shop selling a wide variety of home products, inclusing my favourite biltong.

There are numerous pubs, restaurants and places to eat and an extensive shopping area which provides all manner of merchandise. You can purchase a *Pitkin City Guide* and follow an interesting and informative walk in Salisbury.

The New Inn *(above)* is easily accessible and a delightful step back into history. It exudes charm and character. The food is excellent; you can even find very comfortable accommodation at the Inn.

The Red Lion *(left)* is another inn from the pages of history. It dates back to 1220 and was used for craftsmen working on the Cathedral. Naturally it has its own ghosts, a monk, a lady who was brutally murdered by her lover and a small boy.

The Haunch of Venison is a charming 14th century pub; it is extremely small but remarkably quaint. It cannot accommodate large numbers, so squashed into this oak-timbered hostelry would certainly mean that conversations will be shared by all in the enclosed space.

A good topic of discussion might include the story of a severed hand which once belonged to a card cheat and is now locked away after several attempts were made to steal it. The owner of the hand has been seen on several occasions and is thought to be the spirit of cheating card players.

Three of the many pubs in Salisbury, all within the city centre area.

There are so many wonderful places to visit in Salisbury that you could spend a good few days sampling all that is on offer. However, one of the most spectacular venues that should take pride of place on your agenda is the incredibly beautiful Wilton House *(left)*.

I started off my tour by watching the little video clip of the history of the Earls of Pembroke and their beautiful home. Wilton House was once an abbey but after Henry VIII's Dissolution of the Monasteries the land was given to a close friend and supporter, William Herbert. He became the Earl of Pembroke. After over 400 years, his descendants still live there today. The house was rebuilt into an imposing manor but you can still see remnants of the abbey walls built into the strong structures of the present building.

The tour guides in Wilton House are friendly and informative. My first guide showed me Shakespeare's statue at the entrance *(right)* and informed me that he dedicated two important plays, *As You Like It* and *Twelfth Night* to Wilton House. I read later that the Bard, together with his Kings' Men, performed at Wilton House with no less a dignitary than James I in the audience.

The Earls were deeply committed to the arts and over the centuries Wilton became a haven for painters, sculptors, musicians, writers and actors. Their mansion is adorned with well over 200 beautiful paintings, many of which have been illustrated by world-famous artists. It also houses an incredible selection of Chippendale furniture.

I found myself wandering along the silent Upper Cloisters *(left)*. The walls were soft ochre, which provided an effective backdrop for the marble busts and figures which lined the walkway.

There was eeriness in the silence and I felt a dozen pair of eyes following my progress along the corridor. I knew that if I turned around quickly I would catch them in a contemplative scrutiny of yet another intruder. That is exactly what I did; but they were too shrewd and had swiftly reverted to their previous brooding meditation.

The guide told me how unnerving it was to do duty on a dark evening with an unnatural glow lighting the corridor.

When I entered this superb State Room *(right)* I was so overwhelmed that I had to find a chair, sit down and let the stunning visual sensation satiate my mind. I have been in many beautiful rooms, both in the UK and in Europe, but this experience left me spellbound. Having bought 3 books on Wilton House I was soon able to establish important information about the room. The ceiling panels by Emmanuel de Critz are painted with the legend of Perseus. I don't think anyone would have minded if I

had lain down on the floor to look up and really enjoy this visual wonder. All the paintings in the room are by Van Dyck and his studio. The large painting on the west wall is of the 4th Earl and his family. I didn't sit to look at this; I walked up close and stared and stared! The rest of the house was equally fascinating but no other room could match the splendour of this one.

The gardens are beautiful and I was fortunate to be blessed with hot sunny weather as I made my way through woodland walks, shaded picnic areas and a view of this stunning Palladian Bridge across the River Nadder. Ed had waited patiently for me at the pleasant restaurant with its enormous Adventure Playground populated by happy little visitors and gratified parents.

Wonderful Wiltshire

Having visited Stonehenge *(below)* on previous occasions, Ed and I did not include this in our current journey. However this monument is a very important part of a Salisbury visit and should definitely be included in your tour arrangements. If you are staying in the city you can catch a bus at the station, but a number of travel groups do organised tours.

Stonehenge is part of the Stonehenge, Avebury and Associated Sites UNESCO World Heritage site. The joint "site" covers two large areas of land separated by nearly 30 miles, rather than a specific monument. I do enjoy going to Avebury because you can walk among the stones and touch them. There is so much more history visible in the Avebury area that it is certainly a must if you enjoy stories of the ancients.

When you visit Salisbury you should definitely plan to stay over for at least one night. There are an enormous number of accommodation options available and you will enjoy sharing the city's excellent food fare and comfortable lodgings.

SPLENDID SWINDON

There are fragments of an ancient and historic past in the town records, but Swindon's fame and importance really manifest themselves in the transition from a sleepy, peaceful village into a dynamic and vibrant, industrial, railway icon.

To the enthusiastic tourist who is looking for Wiltshire magic in the town of Swindon, there are bound to be moments of disappointment; but believe me, there are hidden depths to Swindon with its established old town tranquillity, the diverse and distinct form of new, neatly built railway cottages, the theatre, the beautiful garden park, an upbeat Brunel shopping complex, the amazing Outlet Centre, the Steam museum, the vestiges of an old manor house and the wonderful historic Lydiard Park. So let's begin at the beginning.

It is certain that Swindon was part of a prehistoric period in some previous time zone, and without doubt it came under the influence of Roman settlement. Quarrying was very much to the fore in bygone days and there is evidence that Swindon's quarries were in use during a Roman occupation and produced stones for Roman villas. Passing through the realms of Saxon times and well into the Middle Ages, Swindon fell into the category of a comfortable market town, peaceful, quiescent and definitely not high profile.

Growth only became evident in the 19th century, firstly through a flourishing canal system and then with the arrival of the mighty railways. This was a momentous change for Swindon, a small village which had long been considered of very little importance, positioned on the summit of a hill near the eminent market town of Highworth. Indeed the name itself comes from Swine Dune or Pig Hill!

An aerial view of modern Swindon

Starting in the 16th century Britain's railway system emerged and was certainly the oldest in the world. Controlled by private railway companies the system culminated in the railway boom of 1840. This was when Swindon came into prominence. By the end of 1840 the railway line had reached Swindon from London, where it branched to Cheltenham and Gloucester.

Enter the scenario of two major protagonists – DANIEL GOOCH and ISAMBARD KINGDOM BRUNEL, both to become international icons in their own way.

Daniel Gooch

Isambard Kingdom Brunel

What was Gooch's impact on Swindon and his link to enduring fame?

Gooch 21 years old and Brunel 33 years old, together determined that Swindon was to become the new workshop establishment that would administer repairs, oversee maintenance and control rolling stock of the Great Western Railway.

Brunel was the Engineer of the Company and Gooch the Superintendent of Locomotives. However a flourishing and vibrant Swindon blossomed under the auspices of Gooch. He was a dedicated and energetic leader and worked hard, not only in his professional role, but in his duty to the workers of the GWR.

With incredible speed the Railway Village emerged with workshops, homes, a new adult learning facility and all the good fortune and problems which accompany progress on the march.

Workers at Bristol Street

top: New Town
below: Old Town

The backs at the Railway Village

Victoria Road hill

Wood St junction with Croft Rd

Swindon Old Town continued as a separate entity to the visionary planning of Gooch and, for some time, the newly engaged workers were entirely dependent on the established market, shops and services; traders were only too happy to supply the necessary goods and benefit from welcome financial gain.

Very quickly a vibrant commercial centre was established and the growing multitude of workers enjoyed an increasingly comfortable lifestyle.

The Railway village was built with the champagne coloured Swindon stone and still stands neatly and proudly today.

Gooch took care of his sometimes troublesome flock in good times and bad and saw to the establishment of discerning medical care. In 1865 he became MP for the Cricklade-Swindon constituency, a position which he served with honour for 20 years

He made his mark in history as he successfully utilised Brunel's Great Eastern steamship to lay the first transatlantic cable.

It is no wonder that Alan S Peck, author of the Definitive History of the Works, concluded: "His final assessment must be as one of the giants of the Victorian age, both as engineer and businessman, with the religious and moral outlook of the times which demanded justice at all times in his dealings with others whatever their position in life. Swindon itself can never repay its debt to him."

With the incredible contribution made by Daniel Gooch to the growth and advancement of Swindon, I find it extraordinary that Isambard Kingdom Brunel is so highly venerated amongst the inhabitants of the town evidenced by his statue *(below)*.

Swindon was never part of Brunel's mission statement; it served only as a preliminary stage in the creative process of expanding his engineering skills.

It is interesting to note that when a 2002 BBC poll asked the public to select the 100 Greatest Britons, Isambard Kingdom Brunel was placed second on the list. I enjoyed watching a lengthy You Tube video of this engineering giant. With his obsession for work, his attention to detail and his innovative ideas it is easy to see why this charismatic phenomenon was hailed as 'The Man Who Built Britain'.

This association with greatness, genius, vision and fame is an obvious lure for many to pay a higher tribute than might seemingly be warranted.

So it is understandable that early Swindon townsfolk felt themselves specially honoured in that incredible engineering feats had their origins in the Great Western Railway and that elements of success must impress on those who worked alongside and were associated with Brunel as their chief engineer.

L.T.C. Rolt, in his book *Isambard Kingdom Brunel*, described Brunel as "...one of the greatest figures of the Industrial Revolution... with his ground-breaking designs and ingenious constructions." Certainly he will be forever lauded for his brilliant successes in building bridges, tunnels, viaducts and railways.

His revolutionary steamship projects further extended this incredible engineer into greatness and the Great Western, the Great Britain and the Great Eastern reached new horizons in maritime advancement, being monumental in design, size, strength and speed.

I have been enjoying BBC2's The Great British Menu as regional chefs vie to be part of the elite team who will present the NHS with a superb banquet on their 70th anniversary.

Now what has the NHS to do with Swindon? Nothing really! Apart from the fact that Swindonians had been enjoying a hundred years of revolutionary medical care before the NHS had even laid the foundations of a national system; the success of Swindon's health care was an inspiration to the Minister of Health, Aneurin Bevan, and their progressive prototype served as a model for a revolutionary new strategy.

Once again, Daniel Gooch was instrumental in paving the way for this innovation.

Above: The Swindon Swimming Baths converted to use as a hospital during the First World War

Left: The Old Town Bowl and the bandstand in Town Gardens

Swindon has so much to offer the townsfolk in a healthy lifestyle. It has a wonderful park in Old Town with its own amphitheatre.

It also has its very own country park and bird nature reserve. Coate Water Country Park started off as a reservoir originally intended to provide water for the Wilts & Berks Canal.

With the canal abandoned in 1914 Coate became a pleasure park and is enjoyed by

numerous visitors who appreciate tranquil walks or just the peaceful ambience of a leisure facility.

How has Swindon changed over the years? Time is unyielding and waits for no man; thus in its relentless march change, for good or bad, is inevitable.

Sometimes it is harsh, but in the rapidly expanding town of Swindon, change has come with an exciting flourish – the old is preserved and valued and the new is always stimulating.

The Goddard Arms *(above)* was used as the first town hall. Now with tender loving care it has fulfilled its purpose as an historic inn and pub and boasts an excellent menu which Ed and I have enjoyed sampling

The Corn Exchange *(left)* then lodged the new town hall but with the collapse of corn prices in 1880 it became a sanctuary for various forms of entertainment until lapsing into silence for 30 years.

However the old lady is about to be rejuvenated with a £35 million restoration project which will boast a beautiful, public piazza with all the accompanying cafes, bars and niche retail shops.

CORN EXCHANGE.   SWINDON.

Finally, the functions of a town hall were designated to this very smart building in 1891. Times and tasks change and today the majestic building houses a dance studio and media hub with a beautiful library positioned at the rear.

At its peak the rail workshop occupied 11.25 acres, one of the largest covered areas in the world. Has this changed?

In some ways, yes it has changed. The building no longer marshals a workforce of 14,000 people nor does it function as an engineering home for locomotives and carriages

Today, these very same buildings house an innovative and iconic Fashion Outlet Centre owned by the international group McArthur Glen Designer Outlets.

The Outlet Centre *(right)* is one of the largest covered Designer Outlets in Europe.

This makes for very convenient shopping especially during the wet and cold weather.

The whole area is creatively arranged with memorabilia from the old workshops and agreeably highlights the heritage of Swindon's railway supremacy.

Besides boasting over 100 High Street stores with promises of savings of up to 60% there is an enormous food hall and an extensive range of restaurants. There is a play area for children and a busy Hooter Express train which traverses the complex filled

with enthusiastic little inmates. When I am tired I long to climb on board!

No. 7821 Ditcheat Manor (4-6-0) built by British Railways at the Swindon Works in 1950 now at the Steam Museum of the Great Western Railway in Swindon.

I frequently visit the Steam Museum which is located on site. Isambard and I have a congenial relation and often discuss railway and engineering problems. Then I join Ed at the National Trust for coffee and a light lunch.

The restaurant at the National Trust's Heelis Centre

The Farmers' Market *(right)* adds a colourful touch to Sunday shopping.

Much of Swindon's past has been carefully retained but sadly some has disappeared. The once elegant manor house owned by

the Goddard family fell into a sad state of disrepair and had to be demolished.

The Goddards were a prominent family of landed gentry who obviously enjoyed a fair measure of position and prosperity. Although eminent in areas other than Swindon they eventually established themselves as Lords of the Manor in Swindon from 1563 until 1927.

Their home was rebuilt in 1770 possibly on the site of a medieval house. It was known as Swindon House until 1850 when a new designation, 'The Lawn', gave it a more prestigious status. What was the Goddard Family like? Did they impact on the village or were they distant in approach? I expect they were very aware of their superior status as a social class and would be mindful to keep the commoners in their place.

The Lawn from a postcard c. 1905

The last of the Goddard line, Major Fitzroy Pleydell Goddard died in 1927 and his widow, Eugenia Kathleen vacated the house in 1931. It was later used by British and American Forces in World War II. Purchased by the Swindon Corporation it fell into a derelict state, was condemned and pulled down. Today the Manor Grounds are open to the public as parkland and only the entrance gates *(left)* remain.

Lydiard house *(below)* has, to a large extent, survived the ravages of time. It is an historic Palladian country house set in 260 acres of beautiful park land and for more than 500 years has been the family home of the St John family.

The house was acquired by Oliver St John in 1420 and occupied by family members until 1937 when it was bought by the Swindon Corporation.

In the 18th century the family gained the title Viscount Bolingbroke and Henry St John *(left)* received the peerage 1st Viscount Bolingbroke.

The house and grounds are eminently geared to accommodate visitors either for a tour of the magnificent property, tea-time treats, or for long walks in the spacious parkland.

I confess to being intrigued with a little past history of the distinguished, Frederick St John, 2nd Viscount Bolingbroke.

St John Lord *Bolinbroke*.

He was well known for an extravagant lifestyle and had married **Lady Diana Spencer** (a distant ancestor of the late Princess Diana, also remembered as Lady Diana Spencer). Bitter quarrels led to an irreconcilable situation with the scandal of divorce. How history repeats itself.

St Mary's Church tucked away behind Lydiard House must have served the St John family well throughout the centuries, but it is still very much in use as a parish

Lydiard House interior displays

church today and little church notices inform parishioners of service times and activities. Striking monuments in the church are the tomb of John St John, a man

St Mary's, the parish church of Lydiard Tregoze

having lost three sons in the civil war and whose life was beset with constant tragedy, and the golden Cavalier, an effigy of St John's son, Edward.

I have enjoyed visiting and exploring Swindon and visitors to this friendly town will find immense pleasure and items of interest as they wander through this rapidly, expanding metropolis. However, I cannot end my story without mentioning some of the famous and important people who have helped put Swindon on the map.

Arguably the men most responsible for the outstanding success of the railway years were those who followed in the footsteps of Daniel Gooch.

Joseph Armstrong *(right)* was the locomotive engineer to follow in Gooch's footsteps. He was a Wesleyan Methodist and lay preacher. In 1866 he ensured an adequate water supply by helping to form the Swindon Water Works Company.

William Dean was the longest serving of all Swindon's railway engineers. He is referred to as a 'practical genius'.

George Jackson Churchward *(right):* his ideas for locomotive improvement were revolutionary and cost effective.

He took social responsibilities seriously and was appointed Swindon's first mayor in 1900.

Charles Collett saw Swindon in its hey-days between the wars. The Cheltenham Flyer was introduced in his time and greeted as the 'world's fastest train'.

Frederick Hawksworth was the last King of Steam. The post-war depression proved a difficult time for him. Nationalisation of the railways came in 1947 and chief engineers were to be selected from the London Midland & Scottish Railway (LMS). Hawksworth remained in charge for only 8 years.

Engineers were not the only ones to provide a compliment of fame and fortune. There are many notable contributors all of whom Swindon could be proud.

Although Diana Dors *(left)* never gained the fame or popularity of Marilyn Monroe, she was born in Swindon and remained a well-loved personage and recognised as an accomplished British actress.

Born in Swindon, Justin Hayward was a song writer, lead singer and guitarist for the rock band Moody Blues.

Sir David Hempleman-Adams was born in Swindon in 1956. He was the first person to reach the geographic and magnetic North and South Poles as well as ascending all the highest mountain peaks in the world.

Desmond Morris was actually born in Purton! He is a famous zoologist, painter and author. He is widely acclaimed for his 1967 book, The Naked Ape, which was an immediate best seller.

Don Rogers is a legend in Swindon. He was a young Swindon player who brought the town into football fame when, in 1969, he scored the last two extra-time goals to defeat Arsenal 3-1 in a Wembley Cup Final. Although he later went on to play for Crystal Palace he returned to Swindon and now runs his own sports shop.

Ian Fleming said, "There is only one recipe for a best seller and it is a very simple one. You have to get the reader to turn over the page."

Well – he certainly achieved that in his life time.

At his death the combined sales of his James Bond books exceeded 27 million world-wide making him one of the most prolific authors of all time.

Ian Fleming

The children's book Chitty Chitty Bang Bang was written for his only son Caspar. Ian Fleming, Ann, his wife, and Caspar, who died tragically of a drug overdose, are all buried in Sevenhampton near Swindon.

Richard Jefferies *(left)* is well-known for his book, *The Amateur Poacher - Poachers and Poaching.* It is my intention to learn much, much more about Richard Jefferies, a famous nature writer of Swindon. I visited his home recently *(below).* It is now a museum and only opens to the public on certain days.

I have just purchased Richard Jefferies' book, *The Gamekeeper at home: sketches of natural history and rural life.* His prose is lyrical, his sensitivity to nature is unique, and his descriptive passages are poignant. Forgive my indulgence as I quote a passage from *The Park –* '*In summer from out the leafy chambers of the limes there falls the pleasant*

sound of bees innumerable, the voice of whose trembling wings lulls the listening ear as the drowsy sunshine weighs the eyelid till I walk the avenue in a dream.'

To my delight I learned of yet another Swindon poet, Alfred Williams – the Hammerman Poet. I have bought his book *In a Wiltshire Village* and have ordered *Life in a Railway Factory.* Of his many published books this last mentioned was his most famous and because it was a down to earth exposition in the daily grind of industrial work. It did not show the GWR in the most positive light and he could only publish it once he had retired.

Yet it met with enormous acclaim both as a literary achievement and as a sincere and truthful social study of conditions in the factory. Alfred was an incredibly hard worker and studied in his spare time both before and after work.

Sadly, he and his wife Mary suffered ill health. They were hopelessly poor and died within a few weeks of each another.

Alfred Williams' legacy lives on. Swindon should be proud of its literary sage and his great bequest to the town and its countless GWR workers.

Researching the Swindon story has been a joy.

So many heritage sites online provide absorbing information that I have been on a wonderful journey of exploration and often found myself deviating into other motivating stories with completely new settings. I hope you enjoy a similar journey of discovery.

Ed and I have made many friends in exploring Wiltshire and I would like to pay tribute to special Swindon helpers. My thanks go to -

Diane Everett for her significant research in finding past photographs for my writing – the Swindon Society and the Denis Bird Collection for photographic use;

Bob Townsend who disclosed his own personal experiences of being part of the intrepid railway team;

Andy Binks, Chairman of the Swindon Society, who spoke to our Purton Historical Society about the Swindon Railway Works and his experiences – and the presentation of his excellent book *Swindon Works Through Time*.

In ending this chapter, I must pay tribute to the symbolic Swindon Hooter *(photograph below provided by Andy Binks)*. It can still be seen today but it no longer regulates the lives of Swindonians. The hooter was once a small but important part of town life. It called people to work; it signalled breaks in the day and gave the final indicator that labours had come to an end. Life was controlled by it, time set by it and meals warmed in readiness for menfolk.

The staff magazine in 1960 explained that no other hooter could compare, "... their puny pipings bear no comparison with the full bloated bellow of the Swindon Works hooter carried on a westerly gale."

The familiar sound for well over a century ceased at 4.30 pm on 26 March 1986. It signalled the end of Railway life and its silence was a stern reminder that no domain, authority or administration can stand forever; change will happen - nothing is constant except change itself.

But the hooter still works on special occasions. The photo on the right was taken by Rick Dixon when it was steamed up by the traction engine on the left at a Model & Live Steam Fair in September 2017. The hooter is mounted at the roof eaves of the two adjacent buildings

HIGHWORTH
the Highest Town in Wiltshire

Highworth is a hilltop town in Wiltshire and, through the centuries, owed much of its importance to its strategic situation above the Upper Thames Valley.

It is difficult to imagine in the 21st century that, before the coming of the railways, Highworth was eminently superior to the now burgeoning Swindon with its estimated population well over 220,000. Ed and I enjoyed a pleasant autumn morning visiting the High Street and indulging in a tasty breakfast of eggs on toast with steaming cups of latte. The crisp, cold weather made the experience even more enjoyable.

Highworth is a delightful town full of historic buildings dating back to the 17th and 18th centuries. I left Ed to finish his breakfast in comfort while I strolled along the High Street and into the picturesque market square. It was a beautiful day which heightened the character of my surroundings and my gratification of exploring another page of history. I was enchanted by the congenial atmosphere, the leisurely approach of many shoppers and the timeless old-world charm.

Fortunately finding my way around was not difficult and my ramblings soon took me to the 13th century church of St Michael and all Angels.

Sadly, the church *(right, photo Helen Dixon)* was locked so I was not able to enjoy my usual appraisal of the interior and investigation of historic and religious artefacts. The church has its own rich history and was particularly important during the hostile period of the Civil Wars. The large church parapet towers well above the sky line which made it an excellent view point across the Thames valley.

It was a royalist stronghold until captured by parliamentarian troops in 1645. War, loss of revenue and plague played havoc with the lives of the people and Highworth fell into a bleak period where traders became disillusioned and moved businesses to Swindon. Recovery was only enjoyed at the start of the 18th century with an economic boom which eventually benefited the market town.

The London Illustrated News published a report about the church's very own ghost. This ethereal figure was first viewed in 1938, a remote manifestation without recognizable features, with only dark shadows where there should have been eyes. Poor wandering spirit! Was he a casualty of war or a lost soul caught up in the turmoil and sufferings of the town?

I had read several complimentary reviews about the Highworth Hotel *(above)* and was determined to investigate for myself – and I was not disappointed. This beautiful Georgian Town house exudes charm and gentility and I would take much pleasure in being a guest at this well patronised establishment. It is perfectly positioned to receive guests as location is central and access to boutique shopping in the High Street is easy. The interior is tastefully designed, and guests are certainly well accommodated to enjoy fine wine and dining. The pub area is convivial and inviting, and members of staff are friendly and helpful.

One Saturday afternoon Ed and I, with friends, enjoyed coffee, carrot cake and draught beer at the Saracens Head Hotel *(pictured on page 116)*. Later I made my way to the Delicatessen next door to purchase some coffee, but found that they had just closed. The owners saw me with my nose pressed against the window and opened to serve me. What courteous proprietors! How kind and thoughtful! Naturally we spent far more than we needed to in their shop and we enjoyed doing so.

An exciting High Street story is the one that tells a tale of Mabel Stranks, a self-disciplined postmistress with firm Victorian values who was the controlling element in screening 3,000 volunteers destined to be trained as Churchill's secret guerrilla army in WW2.

Once the civilians had been monitored and checked, contact would be made with the Secret Army Defence Force known only as the Auxiliary Unit.

Where was this Auxiliary Unit located? It was only 3 miles away at a quiet unassuming village called Coleshill and in a secluded training area known as Coleshill House.

In preparation for an anticipated invasion of Nazi forces poised on the coast of France, these volunteers from every walk of life were trained in the formidable arts of guerrilla warfare. Their life expectancy in the event of an invasion was a matter of weeks but this did not inhibit their enthusiasm.

Mabel Stranks has been extolled for her role in this enterprise which remained a secret throughout the war. A commemorative plaque *(above right)* has been displayed on what was once the old post office *(above left)*.

Coleshill House burned down in 1952 and its ruin is shown left. There are still the grounds and outhouses which can be visited and are now owned by the National Trust.

Market Square stands by the High Street and the Saracen's Head and that delicatessen face onto the square. Also on the square is an imposing building currently a gift shop, called Highworth Emporium. In its time it has been many things. The earliest records are from a bill of sale or feoffment dated 6 January 1663 when the building was sold for the sum of £100 as a messuage or inn called the Holy Lamb, on the Beast Market including a shop and stables. A tenancy release or quitclaim was sold for 5 shillings in 1690

by which time it was known as The King's Head. The reference here would have been to the restoration of the monarchy in 1660 honouring and memorialising the beheaded King Charles I. It became a draper's shop during the 1700s and by 1852 was described as several dwellings divided between six families together with a blacksmith's shop.

The photograph was taken in 2006 by Helen Dixon during the celebrations held in the town for the 900th anniversary of the Charter granted by King John in 1206 to hold a weekly Wednesday market and annual fair in the town. The weekly market continues but is now on Saturdays. The plaque *(below)* is mounted on the right hand side of the building and was unveiled during the ceremony.

A survey in the cellars in about 2010 suggested that the building foundations were much older than the building they supported. The front of the building is newer than the body of the original building that can be seen behind the roof line..

HIGHWORTH HISTORICAL SOCIETY

Charter to hold a weekly Wednesday market and annual fair on the Feast of St Michael granted by King John to Warin FitzGerold on 20 April 1206. For this privilege he owed the King "one good palfrey and another palfrey". Warin FitzGerold was hereditary King's Chamberlain and held the Hundreds of Highworth and Cricklade.

Borough Charter 1262.

Sevenhampton ... is a small village close to Highworth.

Ed and I visited the church and graveyard in Sevenhampton to photograph Ian Fleming's grave and to learn about his last homestead in the Swindon area.

MY SWINDON WEB gives interesting background facts

about Fleming's association with the little village. In 1959 he had bought the grand country house Warneford Place in Sevenhampton where he planned to settle down with his wife Mary and spend time in the local community. Sadly, this was not to be

as he died in 1961. The country house was in the process of being replaced with a grander establishment. Warneford Place is now owned by the Formula One entrepreneur Paddy McNally. It is interesting to note from MY SWINDON WEB that Ian's older brother Peter was the man commissioned by Churchill to establish the Auxiliary Units of the civilian 'secret army' with their secret base at Coleshill House.

What a surprise to meet the delightful Grania Evans who owns Sevenhampton House which is a Grade II listed building.

We duly took our photos of the famous grave-stone and then proceeded to become acquainted with Lady Grania Evans who invited us into her 16th

century home (with some Victorian additions) and proceeded to regale us with fascinating accounts of her life.

She and Ed *(right)* were very quickly firm friends and it was obvious there was a strong kindred spirit between them.

Grania has lived in the Middle East, travelled in Europe and spent 4 years in China where her husband Sir Richard Evans was Ambassador.

In 1984 he helped with the re-instatement of Hong Kong into mainland China. Beijing was his final diplomatic post and he was in attendance at the Queen's state visit in 1986. They retired to Wiltshire where Sir Richard pursued further scholarly years in writing the biography of the Chinese leader Deng Xiaoping. In 1993 he published 'Deng Xiaoping and the Makings of Modern China'. It received highly commendable reviews and was accepted as a valuable academic achievement. He died in 2012 at the age of 84 and is buried in the nearby church yard.

Warneford Place in Sevenhampton has its own special history. For centuries it was

the home of the Warneford family who, over time, seemed to disperse far and wide into areas of a new world. In 1902 the House with all its contents was auctioned. However, a World War I incident brought national honour and acclaim to Highworth.

Reginald Warneford *(left)* had joined the Royal Naval Air Service (forerunner to the RAF). Stationed in Belgium, it was his mission to intercept and destroy Zeppelins which were targeting attacks on London. He spotted a Zeppelin bound for invasion and he attacked it with his machine gun and expert dropping of bombs which tore the LZ37 in two and ignited the machine causing an explosion.

Warneford's tiny plane was damaged by the blast. He had no choice but to crash land behind enemy lines.

Flight Sub-Lieutenant
Reginald Warneford VC

Now in German territory, he managed to repair his primitive aeroplane and was able to return to his airfield. This led to him being awarded the Victoria Cross – the highest award a member of the armed forces can achieve. Ten days after he had shot down the airship, he received the Légion d'honneur from the French authorities.

That same day, he went to a place called Buc, in France, his job being to inspect and test an aircraft then fly it to a division of the Royal Naval Air Service. Accompanying him on the flight was an American journalist named Henry Beach Newman.

When he was ascending, the biplane literally fell apart. The wings on the right collapsed which led to the plane virtually disintegrating. Neither Reginald or Newman was strapped into the plane securely and both fell to the ground. Beach was killed instantly. Reginald was taken to hospital, but died of his injuries.

I visited this memorial *(left)* which holds a prestigious place in Highworth town centre. It commemorates Reginald

Warneford and indicates how greatly he was esteemed in Highworth. His story is also remembered on a plaque in St Michael's Church *(right)*

The school, which has academy status, bears his name – The Highworth Warneford School and I am sure his initiative, courage and daring are reflected in the ethos of students and staff.

This can justifiably be manifested in their school aims – 'to prepare our students for life in the complexities of modern Britain. We want our students to become good employees, caring partners and parents, active citizens and engaged friends and we work hard in school to ensure that these core values are promoted for all.'

Warneford Plaque, photo
© Historic England Archive 2018

The Vale of the White Horse

No! The Uffington hill figure of the White Horse *(below)* is not in Wiltshire, but close by in Oxfordshire. The Vale of the White Horse itself does continue into Wiltshire as far as Highworth and even Cricklade, which used to house the Vale of White Horse Hunt's kennels with the former Vale Hotel at the end of Bath Lane at its junction with Cricklade High Street. But the Uffington figure is such a famous part of the area that

any visitor to Highworth would be remiss in failing to make this part of the activity agenda. It is only 8 miles from Highworth and the visit would ensure that they could observe a carefully preserved chalk figure almost 3,000 years old and a spectacular view over the Thames Valley *(page opposite)*.

Wiltshire certainly has its own white horses, the oldest which can be found at Westbury *(page opposite)*. Ed and I set out to visit this famous icon which, in an altered form, seems to have dated back through the mists of time to a celebration of

King Alfred's victory over the Danes in 878 A.D.

What a breath-taking experience. A beautiful autumn day enabled us to stand overlooking the Salisbury Plain and contemplate the wondrous creature carefully carved into the chalk hill side.

Another seven white Wiltshire horses are available to the enthusiastic tourist. These can be found at Cherhill, Marlborough, Alton Barnes, Hackpen, Broad Town, Pewsey and Devizes,. Each of them is 'scoured' or cleaned and re-whitened every year by dedicated teams of locals! Devizes is the most recent one having been carved in 1999 for the Millennium showing a continuation from ancient times to the modern day.

Wiltshire is a timeless amalgam of past and present. Scenic countryside, impressive stately homes, legend, folklore, famous warriors, writers and men of genius, all have their own tales to tell. Traditional pubs and inns with local ales and special Wiltshire menus, charming market towns and a platform of world-famous historic sites, are certainly an invitation to visit the area where almost half the county has been designated an Area of Outstanding Natural Beauty.

Bibliography

Stephen Brindle, *Brunel, The Man Who Built the World*, CPI group (UK) Ltd, 2005, ISBN 978-0-7538-2125-1

Louise Vincent, *Wilton House and Chippendale*, www. Wilton House.com

Dr Bernulf Hodge, *A history of Malmesbury*, Abbey Printing, Malmesbury Wiltshire 2011

Sonia Smith, *Wiltshire, Stories of the Supernatural*, Cambridge University Press, 2007, ISBN 978184674 0374

Wiltshire Heritage Museum, T*he Story of Devizes*, Cannot Print.co.uk

Lornie Leete-Hodge, *The Story of Devizes*, The Pitman Press, Bath, 1983, ISBN 0 86368 003 8

Peter Sheldon, *A Swindon Album*, Red Brick Publishing, 38 Overbrook, Swindon, 1980.

Rick Dixon, *Purton in the First World War*, Pixartprinting S.p.A. Italy, 2018, ISBN: 978 1 916461802

Michael Justin Davies, *In a Wiltshire Village*, Alan Sutton Publishing Inc., 1992, ISBN 0-904387-62-3

Andy Binks and Peter Timms, *Swindon Works, Through Time*, Emily Publishing, The Hill, Stroud, 2015, ISBN 9781445642611.

Ben Smith, *Lacock, TV and Film Location Guide*, Parkfold Ltd, ISBN 978-1-907129-18-6.

Penelope Crew Hunt, Mary Brodie, Valerie Cliff (artist) and Mary Breezily, *Dinner At Laycock*, Studio 108, Corsham, Wiltshire 1987, ISBN 0907756085

Roger Griffen, Friends of Athelstan Museum, *Malmesbury's Past, A History for all ages*.

Graham Tanner, *Highworth, Towns and Villages of England*, Alan Sutton Publishing, 1993, ISBN 0-7509-0551-4

Alexander Keiller, Avebury's Unconventional Archaeologist, Pitkin Publishing, The History Press, 2014, ISBN 978-1-84165-451-5

Nicola Sly, *Wiltshire Murders*, The History Press, 2012, ISBN 978-0-7524-4896-1

Richard Ollard, *Clarendon and His Friends*, Macmillan Publishing Company, 1987, ISBN 0-689-11731-0

David Hilliam, *A Salisbury Miscellany*, The History Press, 2013, ISBN 978-0-7509-4111-2

Pitkin City Guides, Salisbury and Stonehenge, ISBN: 978-1-84165-285-6

Richard Jefferies, *Hunting Country Life, The gamekeeper at home: sketches of natural history and rural life*, Amazon, ISBN 9781547245444

Alec Robins, *Purton's Past*, Published by The Purton Historical Society 2013, ISBN 0-951 7142-0-1

Alec Robins, *Records and Recollections of Purton and District*, Published by Alex Robins, 1994, ISBN 0-952 4843-0-7

John Bowen, *The Story of Malmesbury*, Published by John Bowen, 2000, ISBN 0-953 9715-0-3

Published by The Merchant's House, *The Merchant's House*

Published by the National Trust, *Avebury*, ISBN 978-1-84359-329-4

Published by the National Trust, *Avebury Manor*, ISBN 978-1-84359-445-1 this

WEBSITES consulted

www.wikipedia.org

www.nationaltrust.org.uk/membership

localhistories.org/swindon.html

www.british-history.ac.uk/vch/wilts/vol9/pp104-119